Stepping Through the Narrow Gate

Personal Transformation through Evolutionary Spirituality

By Barry Vennard

ISBN: 0-7596-9757-4 (Softcover)
ISBN: 0-7596-9756-6 (Ebook)

Library of Congress Control Number: 2002091732

This book is printed on acid free paper.

Printed in the United States of America
Bloomington, IN

1stBooks - rev. 4/17/02

"Transform your life in the here and now through a new and revolutionary understanding of the life and teachings of Jesus Christ."

CONTENTS

PREFACE

It happened a few years ago. My life started working like I always wanted it to and I love it! Of course, it wasn't always that way. The change was not the result of anything heroic or extraordinary that I did. It was the direct result of a process I engaged in that's brought me a new understanding of myself and a new way to approach life; a way that becomes even more effective as time goes on. That's what this book is about.

It all stems from a nearly lifelong quest for basic truths about who I am and how I should live my life. I don't think I'm very different from other people in that respect. What made the search seem so difficult for me was the way I had come to understand myself relative to everything and everyone else.

I came to realize that any attempt to understand myself would require a greater understanding of human nature. Through that I began to see that people consciously or unconsciously feel insecure because of the inevitability of death. We know we're going to die eventually, and we look for a way to cope. With real security seeming impossible in the physical world, we seek out a transcendent reality. For most of us, that means God.

The desire to know God is what religions—particularly Christianity—are about. What I am sharing with you in this book comes out of Christianity. It has its roots in the Bible and the teachings of Jesus Christ. What it proposes, however, runs contrary to much of what makes up traditional Christian theologies.

As a teenager, I had rejected Christianity for the most part. It was a Christianity I came to know through childhood experiences as a Catholic and later through my family's attempts to convert to Protestantism. Because of my limited perspective, by rejecting Christianity I thought I was also rejecting God.

In my thirties, when my life seemed to be a disaster, I began a spiritual search that eventually led me back to the Bible and Jesus, though not to the denominational or conventional Christianity I had abandoned so many years before. Through reading and exposure to others who looked at Christianity differently, I began to see that being a follower of Jesus could mean something quite different. It could mean seeking the same kind of relationship with God that he had…to become **like him** rather than a worshipper **of him**.

If it were possible to truly become like Jesus, it would mean that a divine sense of self must exist as a potential in all human beings. Like others, I found support for that possibility in Jesus' teachings. For example in John 1:12-13: *But to all who received him, who believed in his name, he gave power to become children of God, who were born, not of blood or of the will of the flesh or of the will of man, but of God.* And in John 14:12: *"Very truly, I tell you, the one who believes in me will also do the works that I do and, in fact, will do greater works than these…"*

I began studying, praying, and meditating on the idea that the divine nature expressed in Jesus resides in everyone and that the fulfillment of this potential is our salvation. That's what I thought Jesus' message was about, and it certainly was good news to me. The more I pursued this line of inquiry, the more it became the primary focus of my life. Eventually, it would lead me into ministry in a movement based on this kind of approach to Christianity.

At the same time, I was highly aware that I had not come close to fulfilling that potential within myself. Even with all my efforts in prayer, meditation, and other spiritual practices, I had not achieved the powerful state of conscious oneness with God that Jesus seemed to have. To my knowledge, no one else had either. And that made me wonder why.

By the time this question began to acutely trouble me, I was a full-time minister. The longer I served, the more the question troubled me. The longer I served, the more uncomfortable I became with the realization of how far we all were from being the Christ.

Was this thing I was trying to believe and teach really possible or was it something we were simply telling each other because it made us feel good? If it was something we were fooling ourselves about, I felt I could no longer stay in this kind of ministry. I couldn't teach something I didn't believe in. I needed some answers or I was going to leave—and the answers weren't coming, at least not yet.

Before making the final decision to quit ministry, I decided to take a three-month sabbatical and undertake a silent retreat and juice fast. I got rid of all my books, magazines, media, and telephones—anything that could cause a distraction. I had a little place in the country where I could remain quiet, alone, and undisturbed. The only human contact I had during this time was when I went to the store every three to four days to buy fruits and vegetables for juice.

The plan was simple: Ask God my question and do nothing but wait for an answer. The question was this: *"If what I am teaching and attempting to believe is true, then why hasn't this divine self emerged in me or in anyone else the way it did in Jesus?"*

I didn't particularly care what the answer was as long as it was one I could grasp and use to make decisions about what to do with the rest of my life. I wasn't at all sure I would get an answer or, if I did get one, that it would cause me to leave ministry. But that was okay.

Somewhere around the forty-fifth day of my retreat, I got an answer. I was walking down a dirt road, and the answer just slipped into my thoughts. Today, I think about that experience and how it confirmed Jesus' teachings about asking. *"So I say to you, Ask, and it will be given you; search, and you will find; knock, and the door will be opened for you. For everyone who asks receives, and everyone who searches finds, and for everyone who knocks, the door will be opened."* (Luke 11:9-10)

In a nutshell, the answer I got was this:

"The Christ power that was expressed in Jesus is God-created and God-granted and is meant to be used at the personal discretion of the individual who has it, as it was in Jesus. Access to that power continues to be restricted because of the potential for the misuse of power that exists in the consciousness of most human beings at this time—you included."

Now that made sense! Even though I didn't particularly like what it inferred about me, it was an answer I could understand. I knew I was a pretty nice guy most of the time, but given the right (or wrong) circumstances I could easily use power to win in conflicts with other human beings. I had done enough self-searching to know that the potential to abuse power still existed in me. I also knew it existed in most people.

However, this answer immediately raised another disturbing question: *"Why does the possibility for the misuse of power exist in human beings in the first place?"*

Was it because human beings are inherently evil or, at best, defective? Are we rebelliously selfish and sinful, as I had been led to believe through my early Christian upbringing? It is certainly obvious that human beings can and often do abuse power. Maybe the Christianity I rejected was actually right!

Again, I received an answer, and it not only changed my life but also profoundly changed my understanding of Christianity and the Bible. The answer was this:

"The negative parts of human nature—those characteristics that arise from selfish and self-centered pride, greed, anger, lust, and dishonesty and support the abuse of power by individuals—are attributes that served earlier stages of the evolution of life through which human beings emerged. These characteristics are not inherently evil. They're part of our evolutionary inheritance and can be found in more primitive expressions in other species. But when combined with emerging human creativity and self-consciousness, they can bring great suffering when they dominate the insecure human sense of self. They are the components of human nature that now need to evolve as human beings move toward fulfillment of their divine potential."

I suddenly realized that growth—evolution—is the true need and salvation of human beings, not redemption from a willfully acquired evil or sinful nature.

As science is disclosing—and as I believe Jesus taught—growth and evolution are natural components of the divinely ordained activity of life. Thus, change in human nature through the evolution of human consciousness is simply another step in the process that has been in place on our planet for about five billion years, the very process from which human beings emerged.

The evolution of consciousness from the ego sense of self (which is largely motivated by self-centered fear) into the Christ sense of self (which is motivated by divine love) has become a primary focus of human life at this point. The characteristics that identify these two senses will be addressed more fully in the following chapters.

I believe Jesus' life, death, and teachings demonstrate that he fully experienced evolution into the Christ sense of self and that this is the destination and salvation of human beings, both individually and as a species.

This evolutionary approach to spirituality launched me on a new study of the Bible, the teachings of Jesus, and the scientific research regarding human origins. What I learned from that study, and through personally applying the principles of evolutionary spirituality to my life, brought me a reborn sense of self and a new sense of ministry. Eventually, it also brought me to the writing of this book.

My discoveries had an amazingly positive impact on my life and on the lives of those I shared them with. I couldn't imagine why all Christians wouldn't be as enthusiastic as I was. It seemed obvious to me (and I hope it will be to you) that human origins through evolution make the Bible and the teachings and life of Jesus much more relevant and accessible than they were before.

Why then are so many people who practice Christianity unwilling or vehemently opposed to considering the mass of solid evidence supporting human origins through evolution? To understand that opposition, I had to come to a clearer understanding of the foundations of conventional Christianity.

First of all, and probably most important, is the fact that the Christian religion attempts to provide human beings with a sense of security by establishing sacred and unchanging beliefs concerning the nature of the God/human relationship. These beliefs are stated in doctrines, dogmas, and creeds that make up the foundation of most denominations.

Even though the beliefs of one denomination are usually considered absolute, they often conflict with the sacred beliefs of other Christian denominations. Most of them came into being long before scientists began uncovering evidence that our species is a very recent product in the long history of Earth. Because these discoveries are so new, the concept of human origins through evolution does not fit well and, in some cases, actually threatens previously established Christian beliefs. As a result, the rapidly accumulating scientific evidence supporting evolution is still anathema to many.

Here's an example. Most Christian religions and denominations share the belief that Jesus died for our sins. According to conventional Christianity, redemption through the atoning death of Jesus Christ paid for the sinful and rebellious nature that is inherent in each of us. His death opened the way for us to gain freedom from divine punishment, allowing us to be forgiven and to enter the Kingdom of Heaven.

Entering this kingdom is usually defined as the passing of the person's soul into an eternal paradise, and it happens only after physical death. As important, it also means the avoidance of a divinely ordained eternal hell in the afterlife, which is the punishment of the unredeemed.

Though this idea is basic to most Christian denominations, I propose that it is simply a theology created by human beings through a limited interpretation of the stories of the Bible. It is a mistake to make this theology a sacred and unchanging truth. It can be better understood as a way human beings have tried to comprehend and use the stories in their lives. Like most human ways of understanding reality, it needs to evolve.

Conventional Christian theology has its foundation in a particular way of interpreting the Bible and the experiences of Jesus Christ, as well as an incomplete knowledge of where our species came from.

"Interpretation" is the key word here—and whether people admit it or not, it's what everyone relies on when trying to understand the Bible. There's nothing wrong with interpretation; it's the way many of the ideas presented in this book were developed. In fact, interpretation is unavoidable. The Bible is so full of contradictions, it simply is not possible to accept every part of it as the literal word of God. The proof of these statements can be found in the many varieties of so-called Bible literalists who disagree with one another.

There are other ways to experience and interpret the Bible. Many people accept that its stories do not relate literal historic events, but instead illustrate ideas. Creating stories to communicate principles and ideas was common in the culture of that day. Because this medium was so popular and accepted, Jesus used it to convey his great truths. His stories helped people understand what he had to teach.

I propose that much of the Bible is made up of these kinds of stories, though there is also a certain amount of real history in it as well. The fact is, the Bible encompasses many forms of literature: myths, legends, historical accounts, fictional stories, poems, songs, essays, and letters. Within this wonderful diversity there is great spiritual truth. And within this collection of writings one can find an extraordinary formula for living.

To find the formula, however, the Bible must be interpreted. All Bible-based religions, denominations, and teachers do exactly that. But some go farther, attempting to classify their particular interpretation as the only literal one. And in saying that their theology is the absolute and final word of God, they also are saying the others must be wrong. This form of literalism provides the illusion of security many people hunger for. It also ultimately proves to be a problem.

Through reinterpretation and an open mind, I have discovered that the Bible does contain great ideas for living. Any ideas, especially those we use to make life decisions, should be judged by how they actually affect our lives. That includes religious or spiritual ideas that come through attempts to understand and interpret the Bible. I think people should ask, *"Does a particular interpretation work for me? Does it make my life better? Does it feel right at the deepest and most sacred place in my spirit, in my soul?"*

As life changes, the usefulness of that interpretation may change. In fact, it usually does. If you don't use the Bible because you find it confusing or disturbing or because you have rejected the interpretation someone attempted to impose upon you…well, that's fine, too. If you're willing to reconsider the Bible, however, this book will be very helpful to you.

In this book I propose a new way of interpreting the Bible, and it may seem radical if you have been schooled in traditional Christianity. This interpretation brings new ideas about the meaning of Jesus' life and death, about spirituality, and about our relationship with God and each other. This book supports the Christian notion of following Jesus—not as a worshipper, but rather as a fellow spiritual being who is searching for a new way of living that brings greater meaning and fulfillment.

Jesus and much of the Bible propose that it's possible to find such a way of life. I have found that to be true in my life. In this book, I hope to convincingly demonstrate that this was Jesus' message—and that new meaning, satisfaction, peace, joy, and even security can be ours by seeking the same kind of conscious relationship he had with God. That's what I believe he meant when he asked us to follow him.

I want to make one more point about how and why this book challenges conventional Christianity theology. I also want to stress the overriding importance of knowing where we came from, in order to understand who we are today, our relationship with God, and who we are destined to become through the evolutionary spirituality taught and demonstrated by Jesus Christ.

A basic understanding of traditional Christian beliefs makes clear why the growing body of evidence supporting evolution might be perceived as a threat. It also explains why a reinterpretation of the Bible is needed.

First of all, Christianity interprets the creation story in the book of Genesis as literally or metaphorically depicting an event involving the earliest human beings. These humans were fully conscious and fully responsible for their choices. They made a sinful decision to rebel against God by succumbing to a temptation presented by an evil spirit operating in opposition to the will of God. They deliberately flouted God's specific command not to eat the fruit from the Tree of the Knowledge of Good and Evil that grew in the Garden of Eden. (Genesis 2:7 and 3:24)

According to conventional Christianity, this rebellious yielding to temptation established a sinful nature that has been transmitted to every human since then, a nature that continues to be supported by Satan, an independent spiritual power responsible for creating the ills humans experience in their lives. According to this theology, this sinful nature requires atonement or redemption. Without that, we face an eternity of punishment in accordance with God's unchangeable and uncompromising law.

In traditional theology, God is separate and distant from His creation and accomplishes redemption by begetting a son who brings God into the world as an innocent being to be sacrificed. Jesus' death on the cross, at the hands of sinful human beings, fulfills the need for atonement. Christianity considers this sacrifice the ultimate act of love by a loving God.

This basic concept has spawned a spate of beliefs, statements of faith, and actions that Christians must accept in order to fully experience the salvation made available through this historic event. In most denominations, the fruits of salvation occur in an eternal afterlife referred to as Heaven. Failure to accept this salvation inevitably results in punishment, namely banishment from Heaven and the love of God. This translates into an eternity of suffering in a dimension called Hell.

In all of this, Jesus has the status of being a unique and onetime expression of God. This theology only works when God is thought of as a supreme and distant entity. Evolution is a problem because it suggests that we acquired human nature through a gradual and natural process that developed through many pre-human and hominid species. Evolution calls into question Christianity's idea that some "first" human beings appeared fully formed, fully conscious, fully able to understand God's will, and fully able to resist temptation if they chose. It questions the belief that humans willfully committed a sin and created the sinful nature that has been passed from generation to generation.

In the conventional approach, humans are fully responsible for acquiring this rebellious and sinful nature. In evolution, you might ask, who is responsible? At what point in the evolutionary process did our forebears do something willful that supposedly blighted human nature forever with original sin? Did anything like this happen at all, or is human nature in all of its many facets something that developed through the natural process of evolution?

Evolution brings even deeper issues to the surface. If Jesus didn't die for the atonement of humanity's sinful nature, what did he die for? Is there any significant meaning to his death and resurrection? These are troubling questions for those who find a great deal of security in the conventional interpretation of the Bible. For the most part, Christianity avoids these questions by denying, rebutting, or simply refusing to consider the evidence of evolution. These are the very questions this book deals with.

The ideas presented in this book are not necessarily new, but they may be new to people who have had a lot of exposure to conventional Christianity. I invite you to consider them. If you are a committed Christian in the traditional sense, secure in your beliefs, you would be well served to read this book because these ideas will become more and more a part of our culture and you will likely have to deal with them. This book will help you respond in a way you feel is right. If you are a searcher and have not yet found an approach to Christianity that feels right, I invite you to check out this approach.

If you are a non-Christian open to the experience of spiritual awakening no matter what form it takes, I also encourage you to try out these ideas. I am personally convinced that the Bible, and especially the Gospels, have a great and powerful message about the emerging nature of the human relationship to this creative presence we call God. This is a universal message, not exclusive to those who believe in the Biblical Jesus. Its truth is recognizable by all great religious and spiritual seekers whose hearts, minds, and spirits are open to the unfolding story of how human beings are being awakened to their relationship with God.

My hope is that this book will support your awakening in ways that greatly improve the quality of your life. The program outlined in these pages has improved my life in extraordinary ways, and this is also true for many others who have helped bring these ideas into form. Be blessed as you read on.

INTRODUCTION

This is not a book about self-improvement. It is not about learning to live more effectively while staying the same person you are today. There are lots of books out there that can try to help you do that. This one will not.

Instead, this book will show you how to become someone you have never been before, someone with the power to live successfully and experience life in a wholly different way. It will describe a proven process in which your sense of self evolves into a new and unprecedented state of being. In this new state, you will become consciously aware of your unity with the creative presence of love and life that is the foundation of the universe. Jesus described it as entering the Kingdom of God / Heaven. The good news is that it is available right now, in this life!

The first thing you need to know is there will be a price to pay, and it's a big one—the sacrifice of your current sense of self. There is no way around it if you are to be reborn into a new state of awareness—a new you. This is the hallmark of evolutionary change. It's what Jesus taught. *Enter through the narrow gate; for the gate is wide and the road is easy that leads to destruction, and there are many who take it. For the gate is narrow and the road is hard that leads to life, and there are few who find it. (Matt 7:13,14)*

This book is based on the premise that this evolutionary change is the destiny and salvation of humankind. This is good news because its purpose is the expansion of God's love in ways that make life so much better here on Earth. Through this spiritual change in ourselves we bring the Kingdom of Heaven into visibility through the unfolding stories of our lives. That's the reward and it's worth it!

Jesus taught and demonstrated this Christ sense of self in the last three years of his life. Through his power to create good and reduce suffering, he showed what evolutionary change could mean for us. We are ready for this next step.

In these pages, you will learn how to apply a program of spiritual evolution to your life. First, however, we need to look at the principles of evolution and explore the differences between the "ego sense of self" and the "Christ sense of self."

The Changing Sense of Self

The "sense of self" is the consciousness from which an individual makes choices in response to the unfolding conditions of life. The evolutionary change happening to human beings right now is in the realm of consciousness. It is the evolution from the "ego sense of self" toward the "Christ (or divine) sense of self."

Ego Sense of Self

1. Physically separate from other individuals and God; having attributes and characteristics that identify its uniqueness and separateness.

2. Has a separate self-interest, independent and often in conflict or competition with the self-interest of others.

3. Ultimate reality is determined by the five senses, genetic programming, cultural influences, and past experience.

4. Satisfaction of the primate tribal instinct for a high and

Christ Sense of Self

1. Spiritual unity (oneness) with God, creation, and all life is the ultimate reality. Uniqueness and separation exist for the purpose of creating and expanding connections of mutual enhancement (love).

2. Expanding good through mutually enhancing relationships is the purpose of its self-interest and the self-interest of others.

3. Love and eternal life is the ultimate reality determined by conscious union with God. The five senses, genetic programming, cultural influences, and past

secure place in society along with satisfaction of sex and survival instincts are the purpose of life.

5. Fear motivates it to act in ways intended to reduce or eliminate potential threats to the satisfaction of the social, sexual, and survival instincts.

6. Birth (or conception) marks the beginning and death marks the end of its life.

experiences serve to make love visible in the unfolding story of life.

4. The instincts associated with biological life make it possible for the Christ to be born into the physical human experience.

5. Divine, creative power enable it to expand love and create good through every experience in the unfolding story of life.

6. Because eternal life is its reality, nothing, including physical death, can threaten its existence.

Where Did I Come From? Where Am I Going?

Some say evolution tells us who we are. For many in our culture, so does the Bible. Science informs us that we share a common history with primates. Christian theology insists that we are a unique and independent act of divine creation.

As stated earlier, the major issue that surfaces from this questioning about human origins, at least in Christianity, is who's responsible for the negative (or sinful) aspect of human nature. Did we acquire this troublesome nature through evolution or is it the result of a willful human transgression against God? Traditional Christianity is based on the transgression theory and, of course, salvation.

The compulsion to continually inquire about who we are, where we come from, and where we are going is a defining characteristic of humankind. It appears that no other species of life is bothered—or blessed—by this concern. Sometimes we are aware of these questions; most of the time we are not. However, the questions are always asked and answered in every response we make to life.

The answers are often fairly accurate and lead to good choices. Every day when you wake up, for example, the subconscious reboots your sense of awareness with these three basic questions:

> *Who am I?*
> Answer: I am a human being.
> *Where have I been?*
> Answer: I just woke up from a long period of sleep.
> *Where am I going?*
> Answer: I am going to the bathroom to meet an immediate physical need!

When applied to the expanded scope of our lives, the answers are not so easily arrived at. *What am I doing today...this week...this year?* Expanded farther, the answers are even more difficult to come up with. *What should I be doing with my life?* Whatever the answers turn out to be, they make up our deepest personal feelings. These feelings become major factors in how we sense purpose in our lives, create goals, select careers, and find mates.

Feelings based on inaccurate or illusionary answers about our past, present, and future often produce less-than-satisfying results. And so the questions continue to be asked—over and over—in hopes of changing the outcomes. They nearly always lead to a desire to find an ultimate truth that brings a permanent sense of security.

Science, religion, spirituality, and philosophy are ways we attempt to answer these questions at universal or metaphysical levels. At this stage of human awareness, the answers proposed by different schools of inquiry are often at odds with one another. Science and religion are examples of that.

Science discloses that we are biological organisms created from a genetically based reproductive process that has evolved over billions of years. In terms of the history of Earth, our species emerged just a blink ago. Science also says that, as living organisms, we cease to exist after the experience known as death.

There are many religious approaches to this question. The one this book addresses is Christianity, whose traditional theology states that we are creations of God, in fact made in God's image. It further says that because of an act of defiance at some prehistoric time, we created a sinful nature that is transmitted from generation to generation. According to this theory, God used the crucifixion and resurrection of Jesus to provide us with atonement, the possibility of salvation, and afterlife in either heaven or hell.

Many people who are looking for answers in Christianity now find this particular interpretation of the Bible questionable. This is partly because science continues to disclose evidence about the universe that contradicts much of those early Christian beliefs.

This is nothing new. When Copernicus and Galileo demonstrated that the Earth revolved around the sun, the church strongly resisted this stunning and humbling discovery. Many who participated in questioning church beliefs were convicted of heresy; some were even tortured and executed. That didn't stop scientific inquiry, and for many this new reality about the nature of the universe eventually resulted in an expanded sense of the nature of God.

Science, for the most part, readily admits that its current answers are incomplete. Many religions would never admit to having incomplete answers, an approach that is currently proving to be the undoing of some denominations.

The Bible itself is not the problem. The problem lies with the way interpretations have become dogmatized. Unwilling to reinterpret, those who dogmatize particular Bible interpretations fail to realize that understanding and access to Biblical truth may be increased—should be increased—by solid scientific discovery.

This book proposes that the Bible contains spiritual truths about the fundamental human questions of who we are, where we come from, and where we are going. It proposes that these truths become more accessible and more relevant to our personal lives when reinterpreted within the context of discoveries about our history.

Can the Bible and solid scientific discovery both be right? They not only can, they should be if the Bible is truly a product of spiritual revelation. Both scientific discovery and spiritual revelation should uncover the activity of the same creative presence—God. For that to happen, a continued search for the truth in both will be required.

The Question of Our Origins

A tremendous amount of scientific evidence supports the theory that humankind's current state began with the emergence of the hominid species in Africa some four to five million years ago. Our future state is that of divine human being.

This unusual and unprecedented change was identified and expressed fully by Jesus, and possibly the Buddha and other holy persons in history. It is a step that involves a major transformation in human nature. It is how the human race will evolve and avoid extinction, and you and I have an important role to play in that.

An essential part of this step is becoming aware of our past evolutionary state. Learning how our species developed opens our minds to a greater and more useful understanding of the teachings of Jesus. At this point in time we are between states. We are influenced by both our instinct-based primate past and by the activity of God calling us into our future divine state.

No wonder life often seems so confusing!

Simply understanding that we are in the middle of an evolutionary process helps reduce the confusion. Throughout this book I will demonstrate how moving forward in this process will provide the greatest satisfaction possible.

It is not an easy transformation because we continue to be influenced by the genetic material we inherited. What is becoming evident is that we often demonstrate primate characteristics, although with a much higher degree of sophistication and creativity than our less-evolved "relatives."

Current research discloses that our closest evolutionary relatives are the Common Chimpanzee and the Bonobo. The difference in genetic makeup between these two species and us is less than two percent. Frans de Waal and other researchers recently found what appears to be primitive forms of moral, ethical, and cultural behaviors in chimpanzees that previously were believed to be the exclusive domain of human beings. This information is important because it discloses that we have inherited much of what makes up human nature, both good and bad, from our primate ancestors. *(See Selected Bibliography at the end of this book.)*

Amazingly, this new understanding about the evolution of behavior helps us better understand what Jesus was talking about when he said we should take up the cross. He was talking about the evolution of the sense of self that is the "Lord of our Being." He was talking about dying to one sense of self and being reborn into another.

Evolution has always depended on birth and death for change. Like all life, we are designed for evolution.

What This Means to You and Me

We cannot direct the transformation process. It is divinely directed. But we are required to cooperate and participate in it. (We can only make ourselves available to the Holy Spirit, knowing that God will bring into our lives everything we need.)

The transformation process can be understood through classes and reading, but it can only be accomplished through real life experiences that are uniquely yours. The teachings of Jesus in the Gospels provide instruction in the process. Embracing the Twelve Steps detailed in this book—*without reservation*—will make it possible for you to fulfill your role. There are also many other books on spiritual growth and forgiveness that can help.

Even with all the knowledge we can accumulate, we remain instinctual beings, unable to change our natures through human effort alone. Through the Twelve Steps we can look to God for the power to change and then submit to the process as it unfolds in the unique experiences of our individual lives.

It will be helpful for most of us to give support and to receive it from others while in this process. A Transformation of Life support group that uses these Twelve Steps can be invaluable. This book is designed as a step-by-step companion guide for these supportive environments. (If in reading this book you feel drawn to this process you might consider forming a Transformation of Life group in your community or church.)

The Twelve Steps Of Transformation
INTRODUCTION

The spiritual transformation described in this book is based on a twelve-step process that will produce a life-changing spiritual awakening in virtually anyone willing to embrace it without reservation.

The Twelve Steps have most often been associated with the addiction-recovery community, but the underlying principles are universal. This particular program is a modified version of the process used by Alcoholic Anonymous, and is used with permission of Alcoholic Anonymous World Services*. Even though this version relies on the teachings of Jesus Christ, the basic spiritual principles can be found in most religious and spiritual disciplines. They have no special relationship to Christianity or addiction recovery.

As evidenced in the recovery community, the result of spiritual awakening is release from states of mind that wreak havoc or limit the expansion of good in people's lives. One need not be substance-addicted in order to need the transformation that comes through authentic spiritual awakening. Addiction to any number of ego states of mind creates the kind of pain and suffering that can be relieved through this awakening. The truth is that spiritual awakening is the destiny and the salvation of humankind as a race and for us individually.

Most of us want to live more effectively, which simply means finding a way to bring increased love, joy, and peace into our lives. At

---

* The Twelve Steps of Alcoholics Anonymous have been reprinted and adapted with the permission of Alcoholics Anonymous World Services Inc. Permission to reprint or adapt the Twelve Steps does not mean that Alcoholics Anonymous is affiliated with this program. A.A. is a program of recovery from alcoholism only. Use or adaptation of A.A.'s steps in connection with other programs and activities that are patterned after A.A. but address other problems or use in any other non-A.A. context does not imply otherwise. Additionally, while A.A. is a spiritual program, it is not a religious program. A.A. is not affiliated or allied with any sect, denomination, or specific religious belief.

our core, we are looking for more than just relief from a particular condition. We want ongoing access to a power that will allow us to create satisfying lives and overcome problems that seem to block that from happening. What we want is divine power, but in our existing state of evolution we are not yet ready.

Reducing the perceived need to use power in conflicting and competitive relationships is what Jesus taught—and it's what makes us ready. This is what these Twelve Steps are about. They are about changing consciousness in ways that reduce self-centered fears, the fears that motivate humans to use and abuse power in ways inconsistent with God's emerging will for us. The result is the emergence of a new self, one that increasingly is able to express the divine creative power that exists as a potential in our species. It is the self that was the Christ in Jesus.

Changing consciousness has been the goal of nearly every spiritual discipline. In this transformation process, consciousness is addressed as twelve separate faculties of mind that make up the evolutionary cycle. These components were identified by Charles Fillmore, cofounder of the Unity movement, who used a form of metaphysical interpretation to relate them to the twelve disciples of Jesus. We follow his lead in this book. (For more about the origins of the Unity movement, turn to page 133.)

Organized into three distinct stages, detailed below, the Twelve Steps address the evolutionary cycle of spiritual transformation from the "ego sense of self" to the "Christ sense of self." As you will see, this transformation is most successful when the ego sense of self is not condemned as inherently evil. It is simply a state we are called to outgrow.

This need is stated in the following two ideas:

o *Every person has taken on elements of human nature as it presently exists for the purpose of accepting and then spiritually transcending that nature; and through that, moving themselves and the human race forward in the evolutionary journey toward conscious unity with God.*
o *Through spiritual evolution each person's life becomes an expression of an emerging divine sense of self,*

demonstrating the glory of God and God's will for the creation of new expressions of love and abundant life.

The Three Foundational Steps provide our entry into the process of transformation, representing the foundation of the divine creative process. The steps and corresponding faculties of mind are: Life, the creative activity of God; Love, the connecting activity of God; and Faith, the constructive activity of God that makes Life and Love visible—in time and space and as our life story.

The Six Life Review Steps represent the elements of consciousness expressed as the unfolding stories of our personal lives. With God as our inner guide, we assess our past and current beliefs, ideas, attitudes, and actions and release those that no longer work for us. The steps and faculties of mind are: Understanding, Judgment, Renunciation, Will, Order, and Zeal.

The Three Steps into Christhood bring us full circle back to life in the world, but to a life transformed. We continue to learn and grow in a stable, serene, and harmonious pattern, knowing that God's loving presence is always there to protect and guide us. The steps and faculties of mind are: Strength, Imagination, and Power.

The twelve chapters that follow are designed to support you in your personal path of spiritual evolution. Some of the work may seem difficult or painful at first. Some of it must be done alone in the deepest and most secret place of your personal consciousness. Some of it must be done in the company of others. All of it will be done with the support of this living, creative presence we call God.

In undertaking and completing this spiritual transformation, you will be making a unique contribution to the evolution of the human race. This is God's will for us, and your life will be extraordinarily blessed as you become a follower of Jesus and give birth to your own Christ nature.

Chapter One

LIFE

*In **Step One**, we admit we are powerless over some condition or thing in our life and that life has become unmanageable.*

Why is admitting to powerlessness and to an unmanageable life an important first step in the process of spiritual transformation? Wouldn't it be better to affirm that God has given us all of the personal power we need—and that, with this power, we can successfully manage our lives today?

> *Life is the generative, creative faculty of mind associated with Step One. It is the power of mind that generates and regenerates divine energy into physical form.* **Judas, the betrayer, is the apostle.**

That's certainly a positive-sounding approach! And it would actually make sense if our identities as human beings and our human nature were in their final form.

But the fact is, we're not there yet. We are still growing and evolving from one state to another—from our current ego-based sense of self to a divine Christ-based sense of self. It's important to understand that there's nothing truly wrong with us; we just lack the life-creating power we want. This desire to create a highly satisfying and meaningful life draws us on.

Golfing phenomenon Tiger Woods serves as a good illustration of this. When he was 11 years old, he may have been aware of his potential strength and he obviously was motivated to develop it. But the pre-teen Tiger didn't have anywhere near the power he has now. He couldn't yet crunch a 300-yard drive. The point is, he grew—evolved—into the phenomenon he is today, and that is the natural state of being human. Growth and evolution are our nature.

1

You may not have thought of it this way before, but we experience "death" and "birth" throughout our lives. They are indeed essential to the process of change and growth. We "died" as fetuses in order to be "born" as infants. We "died" as infants to become children. And so on.

This is true at every level in our lives, as it is with our spiritual rebirth. Outgrowing and transcending our ego self is the next step. That's what Jesus meant when he said that we must be born anew.

"Very truly, I tell you, no one can see the kingdom of God without being born from above." Nicodemus said to him, "How can anyone be born after having grown old? Can one enter a second time into the mother's womb and be born?" Jesus answered, "Very truly, I tell you, no one can enter the kingdom of God without being born of water and spirit. What is born of the flesh is flesh, and what is born of the Spirit is spirit." (John 3:3-6)

In this kingdom Jesus spoke of, you experience a new kind of creative power to respond to life. To get there, however, you first must realize that where you are now no longer answers your needs, no matter how hard you try. This sense of powerlessness is an indication that you are ready for a life change.

That was certainly true for Jessie, a member of my Transformation of Life support group. Jessie, a single, 38-year-old graduate student, was having an affair with a married man, and it was causing her a great deal of emotional pain. She had in fact experienced a number of unsuccessful relationships in her life and was becoming very concerned about her ability to meet a potential marriage partner and live happily ever after. She was also at a loss to understand why she felt so strongly attracted to men who weren't suitable or available—sometimes both.

Jessie was likewise having problems in relationships with friends, co-workers, and family members. She had repeatedly sought counseling and had made sincere efforts to work on her life, but she was experiencing a growing sense of powerlessness. Her life appeared to be very unmanageable.

After we talked, Jessie agreed that she was at the first step. Even so, she had her doubts that the transformation process would be any more successful than others she had tried. Was she ever going to be able to live life—create a life—that was satisfying? Through this program, she was. The point is: Life as the unfolding story of our personal lives is what this first step is about.

Most of us associate life with the biological/organic processes and systems that we observe and experience in ourselves and on our planet. But that's not the whole life.

Jesus said, *"Therefore I tell you, do not worry about your life, what you will eat or what you will drink, or about your body, what you will wear. Is not life more than food, and the body more than clothing?"* (Matthew 6:25)

It's evident that Jesus knew about another dimension of life, one we are called to experience as well. This dimension, for the most part, is not scientifically understood at this time. In it, life is the mysterious, creative activity of God expressing itself as a kind of foundational, universal energy. The actual nature and source of this energy remains unknown to us. In order to discuss it, we will refer to "life" as a mind power—the life aspect of the Divine Mind, meaning the Mind of God.

(Stating that God has a mind isn't as arrogant or anthropomorphic as it may sound. This is simply a way to put the incomprehensible into words we can use.)

Thus, we will say that life is the creative activity or presence of God. In humans, this nature seems to be replicated in the unique way our minds respond to the stories that make up our lives. In this ability, we are made in the image and likeness of God.

For our purposes, we are defining life as the Mind of God continuously converting divine energy into all the things that make up the universe. As part of the evolutionary story of our planet, this divine energy is converted into biological life forms. With the emergence of human beings, this energy evolved into biological life that has become self-conscious and is now becoming God-conscious.

Our individual physical selves are, then, temporary expressions of life. It is the mind energy of life that is truly eternal; it simply takes various and wonderful temporary forms in the ongoing story of creation. Our ego sense of self identifies with this biological, physical aspect of life, and it has acquired survival instincts to prolong it as

3

long as possible. For the ego, death is the ultimate reality. No wonder we feel insecure!

Before we can move on, we need to expand our understanding of the nature of life. This is an important step in our journey to a new state of being.

Despite what some atheistic scientists might argue, purposeful activity is the major characteristic of life in its organic/biological form. This is evidenced by the way it has successfully reproduced in ever-expanding variations, creating new and more complex relationships of mutual enhancement with other parts of creation. Even physical death serves this purpose, by providing the need for new creation and by making room and food available for this expanding activity of life. This is the expression of the original nature of biological beings, the purposeful act of God generating itself into new and ever more diverse forms.

It seems impossible to observe life, its evolution, and its amazing complexities and believe the whole thing is the result of chemical accidents. It is equally hard to believe that purposeful activity and direction are just illusions created by humans. Still, that is what some evolutionary scientists would have us believe.

All life forms are marked by birth and death, and we're all given survival instincts that allow us to fulfill our biological purpose. These instincts are essential for the continuation of species, for the expanding diversity of life, and for the creation of mutually enhancing relationships. As members of the primate family, we carry instincts for physical survival, sex, and the desire for a very high and secure place in society.

However, when human beings focus exclusively on these physical survival instincts as the only reality, we are blocked from experiencing the conscious realization of our own undying, spiritual life energy. Identifying our sense of self with this life energy is our next evolutionary step.

Resistance to letting go of this ego sense of self temporarily blocks us from evolving into our divine nature—our Christ self in which we consciously experience ourselves eternally alive while we're in physical form. Yet, this is an experience we are designed to have.

The reason we don't attain the sense of satisfaction and meaning we crave is because we persist in fixating on the physical expression of life as our only or ultimate reality. With our ingrained survival instincts, we are plagued by fears. These fears grow out of our inability to control all of the circumstances that threaten us, and they motivate us to use power in conflict and competition with others. Our lives become uncontrollable and unmanageable.

The truth is, we cannot control all of the factors, external or internal, that affect our physical experience of life. Everybody realizes this, even if our instincts tell us to try anyway. The most obvious example is the attempt to avoid death. We may be able to postpone the inevitable, but even that is not entirely in our control. Ultimately we are all powerless over it. So if we focus only on the physical reality of life, we ultimately feel betrayed by death.

Judas is the apostle who represents the faculty of life as it exists in the untransformed, ego-based state. His betrayal of Jesus contributed to the crucifixion, and this ultimately led to Jesus' resurrection as an eternal and individual expression of divine life.

Most people have a Judas level of perception within their own consciousness. He symbolizes our awareness of the experiences of life that seem to betray us at the physical level. Through Jesus' example and teachings we come to know that these can actually be the very experiences that catapult us into the next stage of our evolution toward Christhood. Because these experiences lead us to the next level of conscious awareness about the real nature of life, Judas represents an essential part of the transformation process.

Jesus understood this. He knew that Judas' role was needed. *Jesus said to him, "Friend, do what you are here to do." Then they came and laid hands on Jesus and arrested him.* (Matthew 26:50)

Betrayal was part of Jesus' life right from the beginning. King Herod, fearing that a new ruler might be threatening his position, tried to destroy the baby. In the attempt he wreaked havoc on many lives.

Although not at the same level as Herod, our own fears often create confusion and havoc within ourselves and in the lives of those around us. It's a common experience to feel that some aspect of life has sabotaged or betrayed us. A relationship, marriage, or family situation goes bad. A serious illness threatens to cut short or limit physical life. Dreams of wealth, power, influence, and esteem fail to meet expectations. Sometimes cultural or biological/genetic inheritances seem to betray a desire for success in life.

Anxiety about forces that can hurt our lives but are beyond our personal control lead some people to seek comfort or escape in things that can become harmfully addictive. Dependence on alcohol, drugs, food, work, sex, or shopping add to the experience of betrayal because they cannot provide the peace or satisfaction we crave. Worse, they compound the existing feeling of inadequacy and hopelessness.

Addictions pose a serious threat. At the same time, recovery from addiction through spiritual means can provide an entrance into a new understanding of the true nature of life. Step One helps us take a new look at our lives. We begin to see that "betrayals" and experiences of powerlessness or unmanageability lead into the process of spiritual transformation.

Evolutionary change, as we've noted, is always dependent on death and birth. When Jesus taught about our need to give up the old ways of living for the new, he was talking about the kind of "death" we are called to. It was what he meant in saying we must take up the cross. *Then Jesus told his disciples, "If any want to become my followers, let them deny themselves and take up their cross and follow me. For those who want to save their life will lose it, and those who lose their life for my sake will find it* [the Christ sense of self]." (Matthew 16:24-26)

What Jesus is calling for is the death of the ego aspect of self as the ruler of human nature, the sense of self that identifies exclusively with physical survival instincts as the total reality of life. A new identity can arise when this death occurs, provided we stay focused on God.

It is this principle that makes the spirituality of Jesus evolutionary in nature. This emerging Christ identity knows itself in union with God and with God's love, and it also knows—actually experiences—its own life as eternal. It is the divine potential that exists within every human being, and it is the next step in our evolution.

An experience of betrayal may not be an absolute necessity for your entrance into this transformational process. It is essential, however, to surrender the idea that life can be lived, managed, and controlled exclusively at the instinctual level.

For most of us who have an abundant supply of ego-based survival instincts, this surrender typically results from a fundamental feeling of powerlessness. We may do our best to avoid such experiences, but life presents them to us anyway—not as punishment but to open our consciousness to the presence of God's grace and to help us enter and stick with the transformation process.

It is nearly impossible to make the kinds of surrenders required for this process while you still believe it's possible to manage all of the worldly conditions that affect your life. This reluctance to enter into the transformation process when life seems well under control is described in Jesus' dialogue with a powerful and wealthy man who felt the divine call but was not ready to pay the price.

A certain ruler asked him, "Good Teacher, what must I do to inherit eternal life?" Jesus said to him, "Why do you call me good? No one is good but God alone. You know the commandments: 'You shall not commit adultery; You shall not murder; You shall not steal; You shall not bear false witness; Honor your father and mother.'"

He replied, "I have kept all these since my youth." When Jesus heard this, he said to him, "There is still one thing lacking. Sell all that you own and distribute the money to the poor, and you will have treasure in heaven; then come, follow me."

But when he heard this, he became sad, for he was very rich. Jesus looked at him and said, "How hard it is for those who have wealth to enter the kingdom of God! Indeed, it is easier for a camel to go through the eye of a needle than for someone who is rich to enter the kingdom of God."

Those who heard it said, "Then who can be saved?" He replied, "What is impossible for mortals is possible for God." Then Peter said, "Look, we have left our homes and followed you." And he said to them, "Truly I tell you, there is no one who has left house or wife or brothers or parents or children, for the sake of the kingdom of God, who will not get back very much more in this age, and in the age to come eternal life." (Luke 18:18-30)

In studying Jesus' teachings, it's clear he did not oppose abundance. God's desire to provide for us in every way was a major part of his message. Something other than wealth was keeping the rich man from experiencing eternal life. So what was going on here?

First of all, here was a man who prospered on the physical, instinctual level of life. He had acquired much earthly security and prestige, and this undoubtedly gave him a great sense of satisfaction. At the same time, he was aware that death was ultimately unavoidable.

Jesus knew that this man's self-worth—his identity—was dependant on maintaining social position and economic status. His ego sense of self was currently too satisfying to give up—even if doing so would allow him to enter into the Christ level that Jesus was offering his disciples. And he couldn't do both. *"No one can serve two masters; for a slave will either hate the one and love the other, or be devoted to the one and despise the other. You cannot serve God and wealth."* (Matthew 6:24)

Though the kingdom Jesus was offering is the destiny of all human life, it simply was not the rich man's time. It was, however, the time for Jesus' disciples. They had left their lives of struggle in order to follow him.

Imagine what that must have been like 2,000 years ago, walking away from your identity as a fisherman or the lucrative job of tax collector. Giving up your fishing boat, your nets, your position—the very things survival depended on—to follow someone who didn't even tell you where he was taking you!

Then again, maybe it wasn't such a hard decision. Maybe the struggles for survival were not very satisfactory for these individuals and maybe the presence of the truth and the possibility of a new life— promises God made visible in the person of Jesus—were more enticing.

Maybe it would have been harder if they had been rich and powerful and were tempted to believe they could control all of the circumstances that would allow them to stay that way. Even there, though, is the worry that something unexpected could happen to one's wealth. And what about death? But the individuals who became

Jesus' disciples were regular people of their times, so it seemed. And people of those times struggled as people often do now.

Ironically, feelings of powerlessness or dissatisfaction with life are not bad things at all. They are often the only way our hearts and minds become open and available to the loving presence of God. During such periods of adversity, people sometimes experience what is called "God's mercy" or "God's grace." It feels like God is bailing us out when we need it most, when self-sufficiency has failed.

But it isn't that at all. It isn't the failure of self-sufficiency or the presence of misfortune that elicits a special, loving response from God. Rather, the illusion of ego-based, human self-sufficiency had restricted the expanding flow of God's love; breaking down that illusion unblocks the channel, allowing a greater flow of good—love—from God. And that increased flow is always just right for the special needs of the moment.

In Jesus' time, most people were not ready for the process of transformation into Christ consciousness. However, many recognized the power and presence of God's love, through the healings by Jesus and through the demonstrations of God's abundant provision. Those who were healed and those who observed the healings received a sample of what the Kingdom of Heaven was all about, what was in store for them and for all human beings in the future. In so doing, Jesus set the stage for transformation through evolutionary spirituality. That spiritual transformation is our destiny.

For the people who were ready in his day, Jesus taught them to understand and comply with the process. That's why he spoke with and taught his disciples differently than he did the general public. With the disciples, he went beyond healing at a physical level; he taught them how to enter into his joy, how to enter Heaven, and how to know themselves as eternally alive and in conscious union with God. He showed them how to be at peace, no matter what the circumstances of their lives. He taught them how to reduce suffering and how to introduce others to the experience of transformation.

How this applies to you and me today depends on how we are experiencing life. Do you feel fully self-sufficient, personally successful, and in full control? Is greater control what you want? Is your relationship with God one of attempting to gain divine support in order to better control things and circumstances from your human perspective?

Or do you look to God only for reduction of suffering and turmoil during the trials that make up the struggle for control and success? If so, that's fine—for now. It only means that your time for spiritual transformation may not be here yet. You may not be ready to take Step One.

On the other hand, you may be one of the people Jesus was referring to in his Sermon on the Mount. In it, he said that people who weren't having much success in maintaining the illusion of control were actually blessed.

You may be shifting away from a self-sufficiency state of consciousness through your own unique set of life experiences. Your movement may be characterized by dissatisfaction, disillusionment, disease, loss of meaning, or even addiction. Are you ready to make a big change or are you satisfied with just a little reduction in suffering?

Maybe you really are ready to relinquish your current world, a world that leads to increased conflict and confusion. You must ask yourself whether you are willing to pay the price in order to enter into a new dimension of existence, an abundant and eternal life in which you have greater power to reduce human suffering and create good in people's lives through a conscious union with God.

"Whoever does not carry the cross and follow me cannot be my disciple. For which of you, intending to build a tower, does not first sit down and estimate the cost, to see whether he has enough to complete it? Otherwise, when he has laid a foundation and is not able to finish, all who see it will begin to ridicule him, saying, 'This fellow began to build and was not able to finish.'" (Luke 14:27-30)

Are you willing to begin the process of letting go, of surrendering? Are you ready to take the step that leads into the transformation process? It's a big step, the inevitable step forward in your own personal evolution. It is also irreversible. As life in this universe discloses, evolution can never be reversed. And, as life also discloses, evolution is inevitable. The question is, is this your time?

If you are truly ready and willing to surrender, your mind and heart are open to a new experience of God's love. You have taken Step One.

Chapter Two

LOVE

*In **Step Two**, we come to believe that a power greater than ourselves can restore us to sanity.*

Everyone experiences powerlessness at some point in life. For many, it's a natural occurrence, happening at the time when the ego sense of self needs to be transcended so the divine Christ sense of self can begin to emerge.

> *Love is the unifying faculty of mind associated with Step Two, in which all elements of creation exist to support one another through connections of mutual enhancement.* **John is the apostle.**

But considering that survival, status, and control are the ego's fundamental goals, don't expect it to go quietly! Not only does the ego resist letting go, it often tries to reassert itself through habitual patterns of fear-generated behaviors and reactions, usually in ways that have less-than-desirable results.

In Step One we began to understand that reacting to life in the same old ways always results in the same outcomes. Indeed, repeating the same thing over and over while expecting different results is one of the popular definitions of insanity. We must let go of our reliance on ego-based self-sufficiency—fear-based attempts to control—as the way we respond and react to conditions in our life.

Of course, you can let go only when a better way to live is available. An emerging awareness of a better way—arising from the surrender of your ego sense of self—makes it possible. There is a loving God through whom we can gain a new source of power greater than anything we have ever known. This truth holds the promise.

That's the essential nature of Step Two. The problem is that most people whose lives are in disarray find it hard to believe in a loving

God who wishes to make their lives better. That was my case when I approached this step for the first time. I wanted to believe in God. I had tried to believe. But for the most part, I was agnostic—afraid to explore or contemplate the nature of God and how He might view or judge my life.

That fear probably stemmed from the fact that I had rotated most of my life among three basic concepts about a male deity called God. I grew up seeing Him as a judge who would likely find me wanting in one way or another and punish me. Then I began thinking that, if there was a God, He was an impersonal being who cared little about me or anyone else. Finally, I often doubted whether there was anything like a God at all.

When I began to seriously consider the spiritual awakening offered by these twelve steps, I think I subconsciously feared that my doubts and fears about God would cause trouble. I had never successfully resolved them in my mind or admitted them to anybody. So I more or less skipped over Steps Two and Three and proceeded to the Life Review part of the program. After a couple of years working on this, however, my life was once more falling apart. This time it was happening around a breakup with my fiancé, and when the pain became too overwhelming, I sought new help.

Fortunately, I received that help from someone who recognized that, by not truly taking the second and third steps, I had failed to create the foundation needed for the life review. I can see now that the appearance of that person in my life was the work of a loving God. I couldn't see it at the time, though. I only knew that I needed help and that my best efforts were not working very well on their own.

This person became my mentor, and as we reworked Step Two his support sparked a revelation in my life. I came to realize I had not been avoiding God all those years; I had been avoiding dealing with the *concepts* of God in my mind.

I began the process of resolving this inner conflict by fearlessly exploring and sharing various thoughts and beliefs about God. My mentor asked me to evaluate every teaching or idea about God I had ever been taught or had acquired in any way. He told me to make a list of them all—good and bad, believable and unbelievable. My list looked something like this:

God is a judge.
God is a deity who lives outside of time and space.
God is somewhere else.
God doesn't exist at all.
God punishes people like me.
God can help, but probably won't, given the way I've lived my life.
God is love.
I should be afraid of God's punishment.
God will send me to an eternal suffering in hell if I don't change my ways. And it is God's love for me that makes that true?????
God lets good people suffer and doesn't always help.
God likes some people and rewards them and punishes others.
I have to love God in order to get in his favor.
God is everywhere present. (No hiding anything.)
God is impersonal.
God is my personal savior.
Jesus is God.
God's son Jesus died to atone for my evil nature, and that was an act of a loving God.
God loves me and will help me.
God lives inside of me.
There is no such thing as God...
I am God...
(and the list goes on and on!)

It became apparent that my concepts and confusion about God were based on information and ideas picked up from other people, and many were in conflict with one another. It also became apparent that many of these concepts ascribed human characteristics to God.

Human beings are often unpredictable, judgmental, punishing, and hurtful to each other, and these were the ideas that made me most afraid. Because many of them had their source in religion and came to me through religious authorities, they caused a great deal of doubt, confusion, and anxiety whenever I thought about God.

The idea of a transcendent God that was perfect love was fine. I liked that. But I didn't have much personal experience that could make me believe it. And I didn't know how to resolve the conflict between a perfectly loving God and other concepts that frightened me.

My mentor told me—and I agreed—that it would be impossible for me to trust a God I was afraid of. Or one I didn't believe cared about me. Or one I was confused about. Making a decision to trust God was the essential part of the next step, but he said I couldn't accomplish that with my current state of mind. It was comforting to know he understood.

We agreed it would be impossible to attempt a relationship with a God conceptualized with so many ambiguous doubts and conflicts. Amazingly, my mentor didn't see any of this as a real problem. He assured me there was a way to deal with this state of mind. If I agreed to the process, he said, it would work.

What he asked me to do next made all the difference in my life. He asked me to come up with a concept of God that—*if it were true*—I could turn my life and will over to, without reservation. That wasn't so hard because he explained that all I needed was a concept. I didn't have to actually believe it. This is what I came up with:

"If it were true that God was a completely—100 percent—loving, benevolent presence who was active in my life, whose will for me, no matter what I did, would be to help me live more satisfactorily and who would only love me and never punish me, I could, without reservation, turn my life and will over to it!"

The problem was, I couldn't honestly say I believed there was a God like that. And I didn't think I could fool myself into believing it. Again my mentor's response was, "No problem!" Yeah, right, I thought.

Since I had come up with a concept I couldn't believe in, he said the best way to move forward was with an experiment. He asked me to use my new concept of God for the next six months. He said that whenever I thought of God, prayed, meditated, or considered God's presence in my life, I should purposefully and persistently use only this concept. If the old concepts of fear and doubt crept in, I should replace them at once with the new. He emphasized that it was only an experiment, not an act of faith. I was only trying something out.

What was important to the experiment was vigilance in applying the new concept. At the end of the six months, I would evaluate the results and be completely free to make any decision regarding my belief or lack of belief in God.

I went along with the plan, mainly because my life wasn't working all that well and also because it allowed me to approach a relationship with God without trying to force myself into a belief system I couldn't buy. It was more like applying a strategy or particular point of view to something and then objectively evaluating the results. I could do that. I did it with the hope that something would happen that let me discover a new kind of authentic belief in God that would work in my life.

That was some 23 years ago. And to this day, even though there have been a few moments of doubt, I have never found it necessary to abandon that original concept. Before the experiment ended, I was in a state of belief that allowed me to take the next step: to turn my life and will over to the care of a loving God.

The presence I was coming to know as God made itself felt in my life as love. I was truly coming to believe. Through this experiment I took Step Two in a very real way. I know now that I could not have progressed in my own spiritual evolution without it.

Does my experience sound familiar? If you're at Step One and your life is not working very well, you may be stuck in a dilemma regarding beliefs that is similar to mine. Or maybe you have a concept of a loving God that you've held onto and tried to believe in. If your idea about God is not bearing fruit, it may be that your reliance on the illusion of ego-based self-sufficiency is preventing that belief from blooming in your life.

My personal experience and the experiences of many others have shown me that the surrender of the ego-based sense of self-sufficiency, combined with a willingness to believe in the loving presence of God, will open any person to a new and very real experience of God's love. I can't tell you exactly how that experience of God's love will come into your life. It's different for each of us. Often it comes through interactions with other people.

This I do know—when it happens, it will be in a way that makes you want more. Step Two is the opening of yourself to an experience of God's love and the beginning of a new way of life. It does require these two things—surrender and willingness—and I want to emphasize them.

You must **surrender** your reliance on the illusion of ego-based self-sufficiency. This may not be so hard when you begin realizing how little real control any human being has—over others, over the past and future, over conditions outside yourself, and even over some of the conditions within yourself.

You must be **willing** to substitute the concept of a loving, non-punishing God—whether you currently believe this or not—for concepts you couldn't or wouldn't fully trust with every aspect of your being.

You can do this even if you're an atheist or agnostic. Anyone can come up with a concept of God, just as anyone can come up with a concept of paradise, even if you don't believe it actually exists. It doesn't have to exist and you don't have to believe in it to be able to imagine it.

That's all that is required here. If you come up with a concept you can't really believe in, run the experiment I did. But remember, its success hinges on your making a conscious commitment to apply this new concept to all of your thoughts about God.

If you are willing to do these two things, you are ready for Step Two. If you actually do them, you are taking Step Two. Soon, God's love will begin to reveal itself in meaningful and special ways, and you will want more. If that doesn't happen, if the experiment comes up with results that are different from mine, you are completely free to go back to your old beliefs. They will be refunded in full or in part, whatever you decide!

However, if you are sincere and persistent, God's love will make itself felt in your life. Then you will be ready to move to Step Three.

Chapter Three

FAITH

*In **Step Three**, we make a decision to turn our lives
and our will over to the care of God, as we understand God.*

A t this point, you may be facing a dilemma. You've accepted the truth that your current life will never again bring the satisfaction you desire, and you've decided to seek a new relationship with God.

> *Faith is the perceiving, affirming faculty of mind associated with Step Three. It is the foundation upon which all forms and activities come into existence.* **Peter is the apostle.**

You want a different way to live and, through Step Two, you sense the loving presence of God. The problem is, you don't really know how to move forward. Often, this is when the feelings of powerlessness and unmanageability sink in. Life hasn't changed very much, at least not yet. You may begin to wonder if it ever will.

Don't despair. All is well. As evidenced by God's creative activity in nature, evolutionary change doesn't happen overnight. But be assured: It **can and will** happen for you if you persevere. That was the promise of Jesus.

What you will not get is a "quick fix" that disappears after an initial period of enthusiasm. What you will get is a way of life that brings authentic change through very real spiritual growth you can count on permanently.

Nevertheless, a certain amount of discomfort is part of change. It's like being in an in-between state of not wanting to be the same old person, while at the same time not having evolved into the person we are to become. The ego sense of self does not like this because it feels out of control. During this phase, it's highly likely the ego will attempt to regain control.

There are a couple of ways this might happen. First of all, the ego may try to identify the "real" problem—locking onto some current issue about which it feels threatened. If it feels unable to effectively address this problem, your ego will then attempt to find out what is wrong with you and make repairs. It believes control over life will return and success will follow if certain personality characteristics are corrected.

Low self-esteem, self-sabotage, and the fear of abandonment or rejection are all elements of a damaged ego. Many people who are ready for this program have already tried to repair the damaged parts of their ego through therapy, counseling or other methods. Though some progress may be made, these characteristics stubbornly reassert themselves in painful ways.

As we know now, repairing the ego is no longer the answer. Spiritual transformation is. Transcendence of the ego by the emerging divine sense of self is our destination. It's the solution to living problems at this stage of life.

A second tempting solution to the damaged ego's discomfort is trying to find a "magic bullet" spiritual practice that promises immediate and permanent relief. Some of these practices actually work temporarily, if a high level of intense focus is maintained. But after the initial enthusiasm wears off and concentration slides a bit, the old fears come roaring back. Worse, the experience can leave a person doubting whether anything will ever work.

Avoiding the pain and problems of the past and moving directly into a powerful relationship with God is the goal of most of these approaches. But as Jesus taught, the past cannot be ignored. *So when you are offering your gift at the altar, if you remember that your brother or sister has something against you, leave your gift there before the altar and go; first be reconciled to your brother or sister, and then come and offer your gift.* (Matthew 5:23-24)

Making an offering was the accepted way to pray in those days. If you wanted something good from God, Jesus said you should first come to peace with your past and then seek the creation of good through the divine.

Ignoring the past, no matter how tempting, will not work. And there are two problems with believing that it could. First, it ignores the real source of one's subconscious fears and so they remain unhealed. Second, it fails to recognize that the past—especially the painful parts of it—holds secret blessings that are essential in the next stage of spiritual evolution. These blessings disclose an essential truth we must become conscious of: that God is present at all times and in all conditions, despite the temporary appearance of things. Only by fearlessly revisiting the past can these blessings be revealed.

In approaching Step Three be reminded that all human lives are marked by ever-changing conditions. Those who consciously seek a spiritual way to live find that changing conditions are catalysts for new cycles of growth. These cycles bring greater meaning, peace, and satisfaction to our lives. For others, unanticipated and disturbing changes can seem like proof that life is full of misfortune and danger.

By taking the Third Step we are about to complete the foundation for a cycle of spiritual growth and we will do so by an act of faith. As it was for Dorothy in the *Wizard of Oz* when she and Toto stepped onto the Yellow Brick Road, it is through these three steps that we gain the confidence to begin our journey toward gaining access to this divine power.

In Step Two we began to recognize the importance of assessing our current understanding of God. Like everything else, this is evolving. Most of us initially develop concepts in which God has human characteristics. Usually some of these qualities were those of our parents, but there are many other influences. In the Western world, of course, the Bible is a major influence on the way God is understood. Moreover, the Bible, from the book of Genesis to Revelations, is a wonderful example of how our understanding of the human/God relationship evolves.

The tendency of humans to conceptualize God in human terms can be seen throughout the Bible. The Hebrew Scriptures include many stories of God acting out human characteristics—unpredictable anger and rage, jealousy, even fickleness of mind. The bargaining between Abraham and God over the fate of Sodom and Gomorrah (Genesis 18:20-33) is a classic example.

Then the Lord said, "How great is the outcry against Sodom and Gomorrah and how very grave their sin! I must go down and see whether they have done altogether according to the outcry that has come to me; and if not, I will know." So the men turned from there, and went toward Sodom, while Abraham remained standing before the Lord.

Then Abraham came near and said, "Will you indeed sweep away the righteous with the wicked? Suppose there are fifty righteous within the city; will you then sweep away the place and not forgive it for the fifty righteous who are in it? Far be it from you to do such a thing, to slay the righteous with the wicked, so that the righteous fare as the wicked! Far be that from you! Shall not the Judge of all the earth do what is just?"

And the Lord said, "If I find at Sodom fifty righteous in the city, I will forgive the whole place for their sake." Abraham answered, "Let me take it upon myself to speak to the Lord, I who am but dust and ashes. Suppose five of the fifty righteous are lacking? Will you destroy the whole city for lack of five?" And he said, "I will not destroy it if I find forty-five there."

Again he spoke to him, "Suppose forty are found there." He answered, "For the sake of forty I will not do it." Then he said, "Oh do not let the Lord be angry if I speak. Suppose thirty are found there." He answered, "I will not do it, if I find thirty there."

He said, "Let me take it upon myself to speak to the Lord. Suppose twenty are found there." He answered, "For the sake of twenty I will not destroy it." Then he said, "Oh do not let the Lord be angry if I speak just once more. Suppose ten are found there." He answered, "For the sake of ten I will not destroy it."

And the Lord went his way, when he had finished speaking to Abraham; and Abraham returned to his place.

These Scriptures represent several areas of concern if you are contemplating turning over your will and life to God and using the Bible for support. The first thing to understand is that we all—including the creators of this story—have the inclination to think that God is like us. If that concept were true, it should come as no surprise that people would be reluctant to really trust their lives to a God who seems like us, based on the history of our species!

Since the ego sense of self perceives everything as separate and distinct from itself, it should not be surprising that humans are inclined to conceptualize God in human-like, physical terms, that we naturally think of Him as an individual, something separate and even distant from creation.

From this perspective it's as though God is a watchmaker who winds up creation and lets it go! Like the watchmaker, He may be available to come back later and fix things—if contacted and convinced to do so. Intercessory prayer reflects this concept.

Humans often think of God as a distant parent—a father who observes, judges, rewards, and punishes. If things get out of hand, He personally intervenes. Adherents of this concept believe God is a separate deity who watches over creation, especially over human beings, and metes out justice based on behavior and compliance with various religious rules and regulations. These conceptions of God might have been useful in early stages of spiritual development, but they will not serve us in the future.

It's true that the limitations of our minds and our language make it nearly impossible to refer to God without using pronouns and names associated with human characteristics. Thus, my use of the pronoun "He" throughout this book. (Jesus called God *abba*—daddy.) But it is important to understand that even though God is the source of all life and our existence, He is not humanlike.

In God there can be no place that He is separate from any part of reality. Yet, God's activity does appear to us to have a parental familiarity. When Jesus claimed divine qualities, and especially when he claimed "oneness" with God, he was transcending that anthropomorphic perspective on God. He was also transgressing the concept of a separate deity, a concept that was sacred to the religious authorities of his time. He was proclaiming a new understanding that this living, creative presence existed deep within himself.

When Jesus quoted Psalms 82:6 to a hostile audience—*"Is it not written in your law, 'I said, you are gods?'"* —he was acknowledging not only that humans are made in the image of God, but also have divine potential inherent in their spiritual nature—even if they don't know it.

Jesus was possibly the first person on Earth to understand and experience this imminent presence of God. Through this enlightened understanding he claimed that he and God were united and inseparable, that God's divine nature was in himself. *"The Father and I are one."* (John 10:30)

Jesus identifies the true nature of God in John, Chapter 4, when he says: *"But the hour is coming, and is now here, when the true worshipers will worship the Father in spirit and truth, for the Father seeks such as these to worship Him. God is spirit, and those who worship Him must worship in spirit and truth."*

With those words, Jesus is telling us that God is not humanlike. God is true spirit living within and underlying all creation. God is the ultimate truth, the ultimate reality. God is "beingness" itself.

Jesus also corrects the mistaken idea that this God is separate from any aspect of creation. (*"The kingdom of God is among you."* Luke, Chapter 17*)* He frequently acknowledged that human beings were mostly unaware of God's active presence in the world. Unable to understand and know the presence of God within themselves, they could not see that Jesus' teachings and demonstrations were the work of God and not the result of special and wholly separate human powers.

Others could not see God in Jesus because they were not able to experience God's living presence within themselves. This was true of the religious leaders of the day. *Then they* [the Pharisees] *said to him,"Where is your Father?" Jesus answered, "You know neither me nor my Father. If you knew me, you would know my Father also."* (John 8:19)

In John, Chapter 14, he discusses this difficulty with his disciple Philip. *"Do you not believe that I am in the Father and the Father is in me? The words I say to you I do not speak on my own; but the Father who dwells in me does His works. Believe me that I am in the Father and the Father is in me."*

They didn't fully believe Jesus at first and, of course, many people don't believe him yet today. The purpose of his ministry was to bring us into a state of consciousness where we experience the presence of God within ourselves. Jesus is quoted (again in John, Chapter 14), as saying: *"Very truly, I tell you, the one who believes in me will also do the works that I do, and in fact, will do greater works than these..."* It is the next step in human evolution.

God is referred to as love in Jesus' teachings and throughout most of the Bible. *"Whoever does not love does not know God, for God is love.* " (1 John 4:8) Since God is love and God is the very being-ness of all creation, creation is love at its core.

Genesis, Chapter 1, is the allegorical story of the divine creative process. It says that God looked at all that was created and proclaimed, *"indeed, it was very good."* This "good" is the very presence of love, the living presence of God—everywhere at all times. It can be found within every storm in our lives, often at the very center. We become aware of it when we stop fighting, surrender, and become still.

Step Three is the step of faith, not to be confused with an attempt to get more faith because that's not the case. Faith is a faculty of mind and we already have all that we will ever get. The problem is that we apply our faculty of faith to ideas, beliefs, and perceptions that are not true or no longer serve us.

For example, many people believe—*have faith in*—the ultimate presence of some kind of evil that will bring suffering into their lives. By evil I mean that people often believe good will be taken away from them and the quality of their lives will likely deteriorate. That belief, when applied to the past, present, and future, is the very foundation of depression.

Another example is believing that someone else's good fortune must be at our expense, or vice versa. These negative applications of faith cause us to build lives that don't work very well.

At the foundation of our dissatisfaction is the belief that we can gain security and meaning in our lives through instinct satisfaction alone. This is the focus of many people's faith and, in fact, instinct satisfaction has been a mainstay of evolution on Earth. As a purpose of life, instinct satisfaction isn't inherently bad. But we are now called to something higher and must release that old belief.

The very fact of our persistence in trying to make old ideas work is a true indication that we have plenty of faith. It may seem that our faith dissolves when we feel powerless to control the conditions of our lives, *but it doesn't disappear at all.* Our faculty of faith is simply making itself available for the next step in evolution by giving up ideas that no longer work. It's in a state of limbo; we don't know what to believe. But that's good, because this is a necessary step in refocusing our faith.

By taking Step Three we are cooperating with God's will to transform our mind faculty of faith. Although it may appear difficult, this step is simple. It is, in short:

o Deciding to look to God for meaning, direction, and satisfaction in our lives.
o Committing to look to the presence of God within us for answers and guidance, everything that is needed, and to do so regardless of the temporary appearance of conditions in the world.
o Honoring this decision even during times of fear and doubt.

Taking this step begins the process of life in which we enter into a new sense of self as divine human beings, children of God, and inheritors of the Kingdom of God. It is to cooperate with God's will for us to live life in loving unity with all creation, rather than in a fear-based, energy-depleting sense of separation and need to control. It is to construct a life in which God's will of love and abundance is made visible as us and as our relationships.

It sounds great, doesn't it? And it is great. But it requires the relinquishing of old beliefs and ideas in order to make room for the new. You may ask, "How can I do this? How can I give up years of conditioning, years of habitual patterns of thinking, feeling, and action? How can I stop struggling when my own history indicates that struggle is the way to get what I need?"

Well, to be frank, you—your ego sense of self—can't. The instinct to struggle for survival is part of our genetic makeup. What you can do, however, is make this decision of faith and open yourself to the living spirit of God as it begins to transform your human nature.

You and I cooperate with this through our commitment to the remaining nine steps. Fortunately, we don't have to do it alone. In fact, it is very difficult to do it alone. It is in the mutually enhancing company of others that love becomes most real and visible.

That is what most of us need at this stage. We need to be in a stream of transforming consciousness—an environment of trust and love with other people such as Jesus' disciples enjoyed. Together, we will find the divine help we need.

25

"For where two or three are gathered in my name, I am there among them," said Jesus (Matthew, Chapter 18). He and his disciples demonstrated the power and love of God in their relationships. As we join in the transformation of our minds, it will be the Christ, the presence of God expressed in each of us and in all of us together, which will do the work.

Together, in the Unity of Spirit, let us take this third step.

The Third Step Prayer
(Alcoholics Anonymous)

I offer myself to You, God, to build with me
and do with me as You will.

Release me from the bondage of self
so that I may better do Your will.

Take away my difficulties that victory over them
would bear witness to those I would help discover
the love
and the power of the Christ way of life.

Chapter Four

UNDERSTANDING

In **Step Four***, we make a searching and fearless moral inventory of ourselves.*

With this step, we begin the Life Review process. A complete life review is part of the ending of one life and the beginning of another. Most people in the Christian culture see this as a kind of judgment day, something that occurs in association with physical death. Here, it is a phase of our spiritual evolution, marking the birth of the Christ sense of self.

> *Understanding is the faculty of mind in which we perceive reality.*
> *It is the intelligent aspect of the mind that correlates ideas, using history, the five senses, and intuition.*
> **Thomas is the apostle.**

Understood from this perspective it can be seen as a normal part of life, even if not an everyday occurrence. In nature it can be likened to the conclusion of a growing cycle: Vegetation matures, serves its purpose and dies, at the same time producing seed for the next season.

For us, this is a time of harvesting the good that came from previous stages of ego development and discarding whatever would impede the future expansion of good.

One of Jesus' parables illustrates the need to sort through ideas, beliefs and attitudes, keeping some and abandoning others.

The kingdom of heaven may be compared to someone who sowed good seed in his field; but while everybody was asleep, an enemy came and sowed weeds among the wheat, and then went away. So when the plants came up and bore grain, then the weeds appeared as well. And the slaves of the householder came and said to him, "Master, did you not sow good seed in your field? Where, then, did these weeds come from?" He answered, "An enemy has done this." The slaves said to him, "Then do you want us to go and gather them?" But he replied, "No, for in gathering the weeds you would uproot the wheat along with them. Let both of them grow together until the harvest; and at harvest time I will tell the reapers, 'Collect the weeds first and bind them in bundles to be burned, but gather the wheat into my barn.'" (Matthew 13:24-30)

The "enemy" in the parable represents the fear-inducing ego state of mind that exists in human nature. The "weeds" symbolize ideas, attitudes, and beliefs that cause trouble, drain energy, and continue to plague us into adulthood.

Weeding out harmful ideas one at a time is one of the ways people try to deal with problems. But as the parable shows, this practice is not only ineffective but can deplete even more energy. Jesus' advice is not to worry too much about them while they're growing, instead dealing with them all at once at harvest time. In our spiritual transformation, the life review is harvest time.

I want to emphasize at this point how essential this process is. It will take a high level of commitment and persistence, but you virtually cannot finish with the past and move into a more satisfying future without it. Step Four is the beginning and can only be done **fearlessly** by first completing Steps One, Two, and Three.

Those steps—Life, Love, and Faith—form the foundation for transformation. The six Life Review steps that come next—affecting the mind faculties of Understanding, Judgment, Renunciation, Will, Order, and Zeal—will bring about very real changes in the structure of consciousness, the areas responsible for most of the conditions of our lives.

The most important part of this process is accurately identifying the states of mind that no longer serve us. Thus, we will be exploring what most people would call negative states of mind. As Jesus stated in the parable, it is essential to dispose of these weeds of consciousness. So that is exactly what we will do.

It's no surprise that many people show reluctance to undergo the kind of self-searching required here. They fear that acknowledging the darker aspects of their nature might actually generate and reinforce feelings of low self-esteem—and nobody likes that. In their eyes, or more accurately in the "eyes" of their ego sense of self,

28

uncovering these uncomfortable ways of feeling and thinking provides evidence that there's something dreadfully wrong with them.

This is why the foundation established by the first three steps is so crucial. From this perspective, it is easy to understand that we are not reinforcing a negative sense of self—but just the opposite. Those old uncomfortable ways of feeling and thinking are not the ultimate truth of who we are. They are not a permanent part of our identity. Once this is disclosed, the problem of low self-esteem will be removed permanently.

Through the first three steps we have chosen to believe that we are the object and activity of God's love and that God doesn't make junk! Even if we have some ideas, attitudes, and beliefs that sometimes seem to make us feel like junk, we are choosing to believe that this simply cannot be the truth about who we are.

The very fact that many of these characteristics are going to disappear will prove that they are not a real part of our authentic selves. Exploring them in depth will not be an exercise in self-debasement. It will simply be an exercise in sorting out and ridding ourselves of things that may (or may not) have served us in the past. Whatever the case, they definitely will no longer be part of our reality.

In the parable of the wheat field, Jesus pointedly noted that the presence of weeds didn't mean anything was wrong with the wheat seed. The weeds didn't reflect on the true nature of the wheat and the value of the crop. That's the same for us. Just because there are weeds in our consciousness doesn't mean there is something defective in our true nature as children of God. It may affect our ability to produce full fruits of that truth if the weeds take over, but it doesn't change the truth of who we are.

Of course, there comes a time when the weeds must be dealt with. For us, that time is now.

The inventory process of Step Four addresses the mind faculty of understanding at the most personal level. It focuses on:

o How we understand ourselves based our own experiences.
o How we understand our relationship with God.

29

o How we understand our purpose in life.
o How we understand our relationship with the rest of creation, especially with other people.

Our current level of understanding is primarily informed by our ego sense of self. It is the result of influences from our biological/genetic heritage, the influence of others (particularly in our developing years), the input of our five senses, and our level of spiritual enlightenment. The first three steps make it possible to accept ourselves exactly as we are today without delusion or fear. In Step Four we avail ourselves of new spiritual enlightenment and gain a new view of what we are meant to be.

We begin to do this by reminding ourselves of the basic premise stated in the introduction to the Twelve Steps: that every person has inherited elements of the human condition solely for the purpose of transcending them as we evolve toward Christhood. Our need for change hasn't anything to do with being bad or defective. It's not based on the need to fix something that is wrong. Our need for transformation is based on the need for growth and change, a need that is always present in life.

The life review process is successful only when approached from a conscious affirmation that God's unconditional love for us is the ultimate truth. Focusing on feelings of shame and guilt does not serve that purpose and only makes it more difficult.

The inventory process presented here will always work for anyone who has taken the first three steps and will persist in completing it. (The process is separated into sections. A form at the end of this chapter will help you with the mechanics.)

The first section begins with an inventory of all past and present relationships in which we experienced resentment. Resentment is characterized by feelings of righteous anger, injustice, annoyance, bitterness, or indignation. This painful state of mind and emotion emerges in all relationships in which our self-centered fears, the "weeds of consciousness," manifest themselves.

We start by looking for all present and past resentments, and we will identify the part of "self" that was threatened within us. These threats are always present when we feel resentment. They can be boiled down to five basic types:

o **Threats to self-esteem or pride**. Usually the most prevalent, these threats are directly related to our personal sense of importance, value, or worthiness, often in comparison or relationship to others.

o **Threats to our security**. These are threats to anything that relates to our ability to maintain or increase our physical and material well-being in the world.

o **Threats to personal relationships**. These are threats to relationships or status with people who are important to us.

o **Threats to sexual relationships**. These can be threats to established relationships with spouses and lovers as well as threats to our chances of obtaining the romantic or sexual partners we desire.

o **Threats to our ambitions**. These are threats to our near-term and long-term hopes and dreams.

Start the life review with the most current resentments and work back through your life. This approach helps ensure that the complete patterns of ideas, attitudes, and beliefs will be revealed. That is what we want. It is likely that some resentments will come to mind that are out of order. That's fine. Just list them and then return to the process of working back through your life.

If using a notebook, list no more than two or three resentments per page, leaving room after each one for adding a paragraph or two later on. If you prefer to use your computer, a word-processing program or spreadsheet also works.

Here are some examples of how to begin the process.

I am resentful at my co-worker Molly. She is very competitive, always seeking attention from our supervisor and trying to make me look inadequate. She plans things with my co-worker friends and leaves me out. She flirts with Dan, though she knows I am interested in him. It affects my self-esteem (fear), sex relations (Dan), security (job), personal relationships (co-worker friendships), and ambitions (promotion).

31

Barry Vennard

(Leave space for a later paragraph or two)

I am resentful at my spouse. He gets moody and won't talk to me. He accuses me of nagging him when I try to get him to talk. He always thinks he's right and tries to insist on his way whenever we disagree on things. He gets mad and won't talk to me unless I give in. Sometimes he threatens me with leaving and doesn't seem as committed to our marriage as I am. It affects my self-esteem, sex relations (marriage), security (home), and ambitions (how I want my life to be in the future).

(Leave space for a later paragraph or two)

I am resentful at the loan officer at my bank. He was condescending when I applied for a mortgage loan. When I was late on a payment, he phoned and was rude, threatening, and insulting. He threatened to call my boss. It affects my self-esteem, security (money and housing), and ambitions (to own a nice home).

(Leave space for a later paragraph or two)

Working back through your life, you will remember resentments that no longer seem to affect you because of the time elapsed or because the other person is no longer active in your life. But past resentments, even those with people who no longer figure in our lives, are just as important. Here are a couple of examples.

In college I was resentful at Professor "Know-It-All." He was supposed to be my graduate advisor but didn't give me the support I wanted. He didn't give me recognition for the contribution I made to his research project—he took all the credit. It affected my self-esteem, ambitions, and security (graduate degree, academic recognition, job future).

Farther back:

I was resentful at Billy, a bully in the sixth grade. He picked on me and humiliated me in front of other kids. It affected my self-esteem, personal relationships (friends), and sex relationships (afraid girls would see me as a coward).

At the age of seven, I was resentful at my uncle. He took his clothes off in front of me and said it was all right for me to take a shower with him. When I did, he touched me sexually and asked me to touch him. When I refused to do it any more, he threatened to tell people that I had agreed to take a shower with him. It affected my self-esteem (I felt dirty and ashamed), personal relations (if my parents found out and my trust of other people), and sex relations (I didn't trust others or myself).

Even farther back:

I was resentful at my parents. They shamed me because I wet the bed. They threatened me with use of an electric sheet that would shock me. My mother told the kindergarten teacher that I wet the bed. It affected my self-esteem, security, and personal and sex relationships (I had a childhood crush on the teacher).

Reviewing your life in this way, you will likely find some principles or ideas that you resent.

I felt resentful toward God. God seemed to demand that I live up to impossible standards in order to please Him. God was supposed to help, but didn't, when I prayed for my parents not to divorce. Everything good that happened was supposed to be the work of God and everything bad that happened was my fault or the fault of people. God was good and judged me as bad because of feelings that I couldn't control, such as sex and anger. It affects my self-esteem, security, sex relations, and ambitions.

I am resentful at the government. They make stupid laws, impose rules on me that I don't agree with, and threaten me with consequences if I don't comply. They take my money through excessive taxes and threaten me with audits. It affects my self-esteem, security, and ambitions.

I am resentful at the principle of honesty. If I practice it like I'm supposed to, it restricts me from manipulating people and circumstances in ways that I think make it more possible for me to get my way. It affects my ambitions, sex relations, and self-esteem.

This portion of the life review is complete when all of the resentments back to your earliest memories have been written down. Don't be too concerned that you may have forgotten some. Just don't skip any that come to mind.

Now, go back to the beginning and revisit each entry, identifying the specific role you had in creating conflict in the relationship. That is achieved by asking yourself, "In this relationship, where was I selfish, self-seeking, dishonest, or afraid?"

Be clear about the difference between "self-interest" and "selfishness." All activities of life have self-interest in them. One cannot do anything without some level of self-interest. Selfishness, on the other hand, is a specific form of self-interest. Selfishness and self-seeking are the pursuits of one's self-interest, happiness, or pleasure with little or no regard for others.

For example, a marriage is created through the self-interest of two individuals. Self-interest becomes selfishness when one or both try to control, manipulate, or change the other person so they better fit the role they want them to play. This happens often in relationships. It becomes selfish when the objective to fulfill some personal need exceeds concern for the partner.

As we enter into this part of the life review, it is important once again to remind ourselves that the self-centered, fear-based ideas, attitudes, and actions we will be looking for within do not make us bad or evil. The pursuit of self-interest at the expense of others is an instinctual strategy in many species, including us. The motivation for these ways of responding to life is our inheritance as evolutionary biological organisms. We are now evolving from primate human beings into divine human beings, and we must transcend this inheritance because, in its current ego-based state, it is bringing suffering and limitations to our creative powers.

You can begin to see that this is an inventory of self-centered fears that arise from our ego sense of self. To transcend them we first need to accurately understand how they played out in our relationships with others.

The basis for letting go of these fears can be found in the teachings of Jesus, who said we should no longer worry about our survival needs. He said that people who worry and struggle only avail themselves of the limited powers of human beings rather than the divine powers of God that come through our Christ nature. In the end, he said, people whose focus is entirely on physical life will experience only death as the reward.

Luke, Chapter 12, contains an account of Jesus' advice to his disciples as they underwent the process of spiritual transformation.

"Therefore I tell you, do not worry about your life, what you will eat, or about your body, what you will wear. For life is more than food, and the body more than clothing. Consider the ravens: They neither sow nor reap, they have neither storehouse nor barn, and yet God feeds them. Of how much more value are you than the birds! And can any of you by worrying add a single hour to your span of life? If then you are not able to do so small a thing as that, why do you worry about the rest?

Consider the lilies, how they grow: They neither toil nor spin, yet I tell you, even Solomon in all his glory was not clothed like one of these. But if God so clothes the grass of the field, which is alive today and tomorrow is thrown into the oven, how much more will he clothe you—you of little faith!

And do not keep striving for what you are to eat and what you are to drink, and do not keep worrying. For it is the nations of the world that strive after all these things [primate nature] *and your Father knows that you need them. Instead, strive for his kingdom* [focus on the transformation to Christ consciousness] *and these things will be given to you as well. Do not be afraid, little flock, for it is your Father's good pleasure to give you the kingdom.*

Jesus was teaching a new understanding of the meaning of human life and what we as humans are to strive for. No longer is security through instinct satisfaction to be our goal, although basic survival needs will certainly be part of our lives. Our intuitive access to divine guidance will bring us into relationships of mutual enhancement where all needs are abundantly met.

The key question right now is: How do we get there from here? Jesus had the answer, telling his disciples, *"What is impossible for mortals is possible for God."* We can't accomplish the process ourselves. We can and must cooperate with God to have it happen in our lives.

First of all it is essential to accept ourselves completely and let go of our fears of being found defective or unworthy. We do that by fearlessly looking for the exact nature of our fears and the specific ways they affected our relationships with others. We will revisit each conflicted relationship in which we felt resentment, and in describing these relationships we will ask ourselves these questions:

o   What is the nature of the conflicts that arise?
o   In what ways were we afraid of being judged unworthy?
o   Did we judge others unworthy?
o   Were our reputations, status, or security within our social and family circles threatened by something we did or by the actions of others?
o   Were we afraid others might find us unattractive or unlovable and reject us?
o   Did we fear that our family, friends, or social circle might abandon us?
o   Were we afraid we could not control everything that affects our sense of security and the satisfaction of our instinctual needs?

As in the earlier examples, specific answers to these questions and identification of the exact way these self-centered fears affected our lives and our relationships will pay great rewards.

At this point in the inventory, we have a list of all the resentments that have existed in our lives. Now we begin the second part of the inventory. Revisiting each resentment, we ask ourselves, "How did my fear-based reactions to life and to this person help create the situation?" In other words, where did I act dishonestly or out of selfish and self-centered fears?

For the moment, we will disregard the other person's faults entirely, asking only what our own role was. If we are honest with ourselves, the answer is sometimes easy to see. However, for people who have developed a strong habit of blaming others, it isn't always apparent at first glance. Here's an example.

A man goes to prison and finds himself in close proximity to an aggressive and violent inmate who takes a disliking to him. Over time this bully makes his life miserable despite every effort not to provoke him. The newer prisoner will likely feel resentful, believing he has done nothing to deserve this treatment. He will rightfully feel he is being victimized and treated unjustly. If he were to do the inventory proposed here, he would start this way:

"I am resentful at prisoner Bob. He physically abuses me even though I try to be friendly. I try to avoid him when that doesn't work. He humiliates me in front of the other prisoners. It affects my pride and self-esteem, my physical security, and my relationships with the other prisoners."

If he then asked himself what dishonest, selfish, or fearful thing he had done to contribute to this situation, the new prisoner would have difficulty coming up with something directly related to his relationship with Bob. He probably wouldn't reflect that he went to prison in the first place because he had victimized others. His dishonesty and selfishness during his criminal days, while not necessarily directly related to his current relationship, is responsible for his being where he is.

Here's another example. A young woman marries a man primarily because of the opportunity it gives her to create the life of her dreams. Believing her new husband will play the role that makes this come true, she treats him very well. At the same time, she also realizes he has characteristics she doesn't like so well. They don't fit into the image of what she wants in a mate. Consciously or subconsciously she may begin trying to change him so he will fit her idea of his role.

Unfortunately, the bride was in such a hurry to escape an old, unsatisfactory life that she failed to truly get to know her future husband. She couldn't see some of the characteristics that might prove to be problematic after the honeymoon was over. Soon, however, his aggressive and explosive streak showed itself. He began to mistreat her.

With this turn of events, she is likely to feel resentful and mistreated. These feelings may be exacerbated by the sincere efforts she makes to please him. She would write:

"I am resentful toward my husband. He verbally and physically abuses me whenever he gets in a bad mood. He does not value my efforts to make our marriage work, and the harder I try the more distant or abusive he gets. It threatens my self-esteem, security, sexual relations (with him), and ambitions."

In this inventory process, she will likely have a hard time seeing any personal responsibility for the abuse. She will cite his mean nature, saying he is the one who gets unreasonably angry and abusive; she is the victim.

That is likely to be true. But by being honest with herself, she will find that her fear-based and primarily self-centered motives in the very beginning were largely responsible for her being in this relationship. It could be that her fear of never finding a husband led her to accept this man's proposal. This fear could also have kept her from getting to know him well enough before marriage and also kept her from effectively dealing with his anger when it was first revealed. It may also be responsible for keeping her from escaping this unsatisfactory situation. Seeing oneself as a victim makes it possible to feel morally or ethically superior while placing responsibility on someone else.

Certainly there are exceptions. By simply being in a certain place at a certain time, it's possible to be the unwitting victim of a criminal act. No reasonable person would argue that the victims of the Holocaust or the September 11, 2001, terrorist attacks did something selfish or self-centered that brought them into that circumstance.

This form of inventory is intended primarily for our personal relationships. It is intended to help us understand and identify our role in creating them and, through that, to take greater responsibility for our lives. Identifying the ways we contribute to situations in which we experience resentment will provide some of the most valuable information we can ever discover about ourselves. It will be the key to our freedom and our transformation.

These are difficult questions, but faith in God's love will see us through. It allows us to look fearlessly at ourselves. We no longer have to hide from our own fears or worry that we will be found defective and incur some form of divine wrath or, even worse, abandonment. We can accept ourselves as God accepts us, without blame or shame.

Accepting the principle that we are not inherently bad even though we act in ways that sometimes bring suffering, we are free to continue on the path of spiritual evolution. The understanding we gain about ourselves and our relationships during Step Four will be essential as we continue to build transformed lives from the foundation of the divine presence of life, love, and faith within us.

Writing your inventory may seem extraordinarily difficult at first, but write it down you must. In putting words on paper we demonstrate a new degree of fearlessness and a new step of faith. Love, rather than shame, guilt, fear, or resentment, is the ultimate reality of our lives. As we complete Step Four, we begin to sense new freedom and power. We are becoming free to forgive past judgments of others and ourselves.

Fourth Step Inventory

Beginning with current or most recent conflicts and going all the way back through your life, make a list of people you felt resentful at, what they did, and how it affected you. When the list is complete, proceed to Part II, revisiting the list and identifying your specific role in creating conflict in the relationship.

Part I

I am resentful toward _____

Description of injustice or wrong I felt _____

It affected my _____
(Pride/Self-Esteem, Personal Relations, Sex Relations, Ambitions, Security)

Part II:

Specific ways my own insecurities have manifested themselves in this relationship:

_____

_____

_____

_____

(Answer questions such as: Where have I attempted to manipulate or control the emotions, actions, or perceptions of the other person in order to insure my self-interest? Where have I been fear-driven? In what specific ways have I acted selfishly, fearfully, and/or dishonestly in my attempts to control the conditions of the relationship and/or my life?)

Chapter Five

JUDGMENT

*In **Step Five**, we admit to God, ourselves, and another person the exact nature of our wrongs.*

In John 7:24, Jesus said: *"Do not judge by appearances, but judge with right judgment."* It is in wise and right judgment that we have the chance to be happy, joyous, and free. This is God's will for us, Jesus said, and through our efforts in the transformation process we are claiming that freedom now.

> *Judgment is the faculty of mind by which we appraise, evaluate, and discriminate in order to make choices. In the limited human expression, the intellect and the emotions are masters of the faculty of judgment. In the divine expression, spiritual discernment through intuition is the final authority.*
> **James, son of Zebedee, is the apostle.**

In Step Four we inventoried how we understood ourselves and our relationships with others. That was the beginning of the Life Review, in which we will fully realize how much our sense of self and reactions to life come from our biological or genetic inheritance.

This ego sense of self is the major factor in the way we judge ourselves and others. As our sense of self changes, so does our judgment—and so does our life. An increase in our mind's capacity to evaluate, judge, or discern from a consciousness of our Christ nature is our destination.

In Step Five, we will be dealing with the mind faculty of judgment from two points of view: first considering the perspective of "judgment day" and then considering how judgment affects the choices we make in our daily lives.

The concept of judgment has always been an important aspect of Christianity. Most traditional Christian theologies forecast an end of time and a final judgment day. According to those theologies, all people will be judged based on the way they lived their lives. Those who are judged worthy and are "saved" will spend eternity in paradise with God. Those judged unworthy will spend eternity separate from God in a state of unremitting punishment.

That's what I was taught as a child—and what a frightening thought it is! I was told that if I didn't live a Christian life as determined by religious authorities, I would get to be the "weenie at the eternal weenie roast." The intention, I believe, was to scare the "hell" right out of me so I would commit myself to Christianity and be saved. But it didn't work for me!

Escaping eternal damnation has always been one of the major motivating factors in much of Christianity. As discussed earlier, it is based on a theology that says all human beings reside in a sinful state and that an act of providence is needed to accomplish the redemption. God is the redeeming authority, the final and absolute judge.

According to this theology, each individual chooses whether or not to accept the salvation of God. We accept it through repentance, confession, forgiveness, and/or acceptance of Jesus' death on the cross as the redeeming act that paid for our sinful nature. We learn the verdict on the final Judgment Day.

This particular way of understanding judgment day originated through a consciousness created by limited human experience. The need for a judgment day is legitimate, but its nature is as misunderstood as the nature of the Kingdom of God.

This kingdom, as noted earlier, is not a reward that comes after death but is instead a present-day possibility. It is a transformation of the human mind into ever-greater consciousness of its union of love with God and all creation.

Jesus understood the need for a judgment day in order for that to happen. He understood the need for an experience that would free us of the instinct-based fears that control much of human life and rule human consciousness. *"Now is the judgment of this world; now the ruler of this world will be driven out. And I, when I am lifted up from the earth, will draw all people to myself."* (John 12:31,32)

In Christianity judgment day is usually associated with the end of a life. In recent years, many people have written about "near-death experiences" and have told how they encountered some form of judgment or life review. It's an age-old adage that your life passes before your eyes when death seems eminent.

Even those who don't practice the Christian idea of a judgment day associated with the end of time believe that our individual experience of death will bring a time of judgment. Dannion Brinkley, co-author of the best-selling book *Saved by the Light,* described a personal near-death experience in an article for *The Daily Word* magazine.

"The single most important part of my near-death experience was what I call a panoramic life review. I saw and experienced again everything I had ever done in my life, but this time I literally became every person I had encountered. And most important, I felt the direct results of my interaction with each person as if I were that person.

I was a bully for most of my life. I fought in wars and worked in government operations in various capacities. Being nice to people was simply not a part of my personality profile.

Yet I had an opportunity, through the near-death experience, to see what damage I had done, and that vision dramatically changed the way I live my life. I realized that there is justice, fairness, and righteousness."

Importantly, Brinkley relates that this near-death experience and life review were done in an atmosphere of complete and unconditional love. The threat of punishment was not present.

Perfect justice was, and always will be, a part of reconciling one's life. In Brinkley's case he remained in the world and lived in a way consistent with his transformation, and he was able to undo much of the damage previously done. As we will see in future steps, undoing damage makes this unconditional love real to us and releases us from the negative consequences of the "law of cause and effect."

This law says that one cannot deliberately hurt another without drawing an equal hurt to oneself. Conversely, you can never act truly loving toward another without calling an equal or greater experience of love to yourself. Love is always present, always waiting to respond in a way true to its nature.

The Golden Rule—"Do unto others as you would have them do unto you"—is the Biblical teaching that recognizes the law of cause and effect. Despite this, many people consider the concept of unconditional love without punishment as dangerous. They believe it implies impunity for people who, free of punishment, will certainly continue to commit deliberate wrongs. Seen this way, unconditional love may seem to support bad behavior by helping perpetrators believe they can "get away with it." In truth, resisting the spiritual evolution of the soul through behavior that harms others will always result in the negative consequences of the law of cause and effect.

The good news Jesus brought is that a consciousness that evolves into the divine awareness of love needs no longer fear the law of cause and effect. In John 5:24, he says, *"Very truly, I tell you, anyone who hears my word and believes him who sent me has eternal life, and does not come under judgment, but has passed from death to life."*

God's love is always present to bring forgiveness and redemption whenever it is recognized as the paramount truth. When Dannion Brinkley experienced his life from the perspective of another person—which comes through an awareness of the unity of all life— he gained awareness that love is the truth of life. You might say he was born again. From outward appearances, it would be hard to determine that anything at all had happened. It was his heart and mind that were transformed, and this personal "judgment day" experience was an essential element in the transformation.

Transformation of our own hearts and minds is what spiritual growth is all about. According to Unity movement cofounder Charles Fillmore, Biblical references to **the** judgment day can also be correctly translated to mean **a** judgment day. This translation would be consistent with Brinkley's experience. It would also be consistent with the experience of many other people who, through life-threatening experience or major dissatisfaction with their lives, have "judged" themselves and experienced huge changes in values and beliefs.

Their experiences indicate that all humans have the power to enter into a time of judgment at any point in time. It doesn't require a disaster or great threat. It only requires a willingness and commitment to the process of transformation and, more specifically, being committed to completing an authentic life review.

As Jesus said, we need to be born again, to live another kind of life. Doing that requires us to judge aspects of our belief system in order to determine what works and what doesn't. Our judgment day can be any day and every day as we embark on this journey of growth.

In approaching the idea of judgment, we will use Jesus' teachings and the Bible. That means we need to deal with the Christian ideas of fire and hell because they are part of Jesus' teachings as they relate to judgment.

Jesus' references to fire have usually been interpreted to mean punishment. In Matthew, Chapter 5, he says: "*...But I say to you that if you are angry with a brother or sister, you will be liable to judgment; and if you insult a brother or sister, you will be liable to the council; and if you say, 'You fool,' you will be liable to the hell of fire.*"

In this passage, he is describing how human beings relate to each other in fear-based, competitive, and conflicting ways in order to achieve dominance or superiority. The "hell of fire" is often interpreted as punishment, and this is one of the great errors of Christianity. Fire is not about punishment for mistakes.

To understand that, we need to see the way Jesus metaphorically referred to fire as it was used in his day. One of the most common uses of fire was to purify metals. Another was to burn discarded things. Dumps on the outskirts of cities always had a fire burning; that's how citizens got rid of rubbish.

In Matthew, Jesus uses fruit trees and fire to symbolize ideas and beliefs that either bear fruit in our lives or don't and should be discarded. *"You will know them by their fruits. Are grapes gathered from thorns, or figs from thistles? In the same way, every good tree bears good fruit, but the bad tree bears bad fruit. A good tree cannot bear bad fruit, nor can a bad tree bear good fruit. Every tree that does not bear good fruit is cut down and thrown into the fire."* (Matthew 7:16)

It's clear from this example that fire is not punishment, but a means of disposal. In this way it represents the spiritual process by which sin would be dealt with. It is not about burning up people in a place called hell.

John the Baptist used the fire metaphor as it relates to the process of metal purification. In Luke, Chapter 3, he says: *"I baptize you with water; but one who is more powerful than I is coming; I am not worthy to untie the thong of his sandals. He will baptize you with the Holy Spirit and fire."*

Submitting to the purification process opens us to a new experience of the power and love of God in our lives. There is no eternal punishment by fire. There is, however, an eternal spiritual fire, and it provides the means for shedding ideas and beliefs that impede our progress toward the promised kingdom.

In Step Four we began the process of a life review. In Step Five we continue it by gaining a new judgment of ourselves and our lives. An essential part of this review is sharing with another person our ego-based ideas, beliefs, attitudes, and experiences. We do this in order to find the physical presence of love—which was so much a part of Dannion Brinkley's experience—in our own experience of life.

Brinkley found that level of love by sharing himself with the world through his writings. He probably did so on a very personal basis as well. Being willing to expose those parts of his life that didn't work, he gained a greater capacity for creating good in his life and new trust in the world. We must also experience new trust in life and in the world. This is why this step requires us to share the exact nature of our wrongs with another person and with God.

The first and most important factor is choosing the right person to share this soul-baring step with. This person must be fully capable of recognizing the difference between "wrong" and "bad."

Most of us need no help in judging ourselves bad or unworthy; we have mistakenly done enough of that on our own. What we need is a loving relationship in which we can reveal ourselves completely in trust and confidence. Most of all, it must be an environment of unconditional love, based on the truth that everything God created is very good so we cannot possibly be truly bad.

Certainly there are things we feel, think, and do that are not good for us or for others. But the real nature of our wrongs is hanging onto things that are not working in our lives and in our relationships with others. We resist exposing those feelings and beliefs to others for fear they will also judge us bad, confirming our sense of unworthiness.

That can make this feel like a very risky step. But fear not. We have turned our lives and will over to God. When we are fully ready to take this step, God will provide the exact right person at the exact right time! As Jesus said, *"Ask and you will find."*

The right person may be a counselor, minister, another person sharing this spiritual journey, or a personal friend. It should never be someone who could be harmed in any way by our disclosures. It should never be someone who is emotionally or materially involved in the conflicts of our lives. It should be someone who will love us and yet remain unaffected by what we reveal about ourselves and our relationships with others. The best person is someone who can listen and understand but not try to "fix" us.

Completing this part of the life review process, we begin to see our life in a different way. In the world of appearances, our fears had certainly seemed valid. In Step Five, however, we learn there is another choice. Allowing our hearts rather than our intellect to control the faculty of judgment, and doing so in faith and confidence in the presence of divine love, we can set fear aside and make decisions in line with the will of God.

Victor Frankl lived according to this truth while a prisoner in one of the Nazi death camps. His five senses told him of the horror and hopelessness of his situation at Auschwitz, but he refused to make that his ultimate reality. His heart told him something else—that God was present everywhere and love was always possible, that he could rise above feelings of hatred.

This ability to transcend such horrible circumstances seems almost unthinkable. But Jesus said the divine power of the Christ, which is ours by inheritance, could be claimed at any time in any place. He said it required certain conditions of mind, one of which was forgiveness of others and refusal to hate those who appear to be our enemies.

"You have heard that it was said, 'You shall love your neighbor and hate your enemy.' But I say to you, Love your enemies and pray for those who persecute you, so that you may be children of your Father in heaven; for he makes his sun rise on the evil and on the good, and sends rain on the righteous and on the unrighteous." (Matthew 5:43-45)

Victor Frankl was a Jew, not a Christian, but he understood those conditions. He let his heart have mastery over his faculty of judgment.

Nazi death camps were the ultimate expression of un-evolved, primate-based human will—focused on the tribal instinct to control and dominate others and immersed in the mentality of survival of the fittest. As history discloses, it backfired. Resistance to evolution always does.

The Nazi philosophy was based on the tribal idea that the Aryan race was born superior to all other races and that the Jewish race, in particular, was inherently unworthy. World domination and extermination of the Jews were attempts by the Aryans to secure their superior position. This is an instinctual component of the primate animal world. It goes without saying that acting out this stage of primate evolution is no longer acceptable for human beings.

The Nazis caused much suffering for others and ultimately for themselves. In a physical sense, Victor Frankl was quite powerless over those who had judged him unworthy. But as demonstrated, he was not powerless over the inner circumstances of his being. He simply would not allow his fear to degenerate into resentment and hate.

That commitment to truth resulted in the increased presence of love in his conscious mind and subsequently in his life. He survived the seemingly unsurvivable, becoming an inspiration to people around the world and a real power in helping humanity free itself from the insanity of the Nazi tribal mentality.

Through Step Five we begin to discard many of the beliefs inherited through our culture and genetic/biological evolution. By sharing our experiences with another, the hidden patterns of painful conflict created by our self-centered fears are revealed. We see that our faculty of judgment—our capacity for true wisdom—was enslaved to the intellect and the emotions, to our limited ego-based understanding of life. As we gain a new wisdom through the life review steps, we see how our intellect and emotions become the servants, rather than the lords, of our being.

The intellect and the five senses now serve as observers of the conditions of life and inform the intuitive self, the heart. Increasingly aware of its unity with God, the heart of the individual becomes the master through the truth of life.

Once we reveal everything about ourselves to another human being, keeping no secrets and withholding nothing, we become more aware that we are inherently worthy. We begin a new experience of life as we enter into a consciousness of the Kingdom of God.

We began to realize this in Steps One through Four. In Step Five this realization begins to be expressed in the outer circumstances of our lives. Love and trust begin to replace the fears of unworthiness and death. A new and welcome power becomes more active in our lives and we are grateful.

Our transformation is underway, and it feels good. But there is more to do. Steps Six and Seven deal with the mind powers of renunciation and will. Knowing that we are loved and that God can never be anything less than completely and utterly devoted to our well-being, we will submit ourselves to the purifying fire of the Holy Spirit as It removes from us that which is no longer useful.

Chapter Six

RENUNCIATION

> *In **Step Six**, we are entirely ready to have God remove all of our limiting beliefs.*

During Steps Four and Five, we inventoried and shared with God and another human being the ideas, attitudes, and beliefs that cause many of the problems in our lives and our relationships with others. These are the components of our ego sense of self that will be transformed through spiritual evolution. The next step is to activate the mind faculty of renunciation and apply it to the specific self-centered fears that drive those troublesome belief systems.

> *Renunciation is the faculty of mind in which a decision is made to release the previous focus of conscious mind energy in order to make it available for the new.*
>
> **Thaddeaus is the apostle.**

It is important to attain a clear understanding of these fear-based components. A very helpful way of doing so is by listing them. In making the list, we again remind ourselves that we are not bad or defective people.

What we've discovered within ourselves are simply fear-driven strategies of life inherited as part of our human nature. They were mostly acquired during developmental years. We are now coming to realize how limited they are and how much pain they cause when we try to hang onto them. The discomfort is the result of God's calling us to expand our capacity for successful living.

Because of that we are choosing to release these personal and limiting strategies. As disclosed in Step Five, true release can only be accomplished through acceptance, not condemnation. Jesus taught that judgmental condemnation of ourselves and others severely reduces our capacity to let go and change.

Before continuing with Step Six, let's look at some of the more common ways self-centered fear manifests itself. These characteristics can become powerful influences on our personalities because of the conscious or subconscious belief that they have payoffs.

Low Self-Esteem

This condition is usually acquired during childhood, with individuals believing or suspecting there is something inherently wrong, defective, or unworthy about themselves. Typically they try to compensate by seeking attention, recognition, and validation from others. If this cannot be done in positive ways, they try negative validation because even this is preferable to being ignored.

Low self-esteem conflicts with the ego's desire to be recognized as valuable and worthy. Always remember that development of the ego is an essential part of the human journey. Because of the fear that acknowledging low self-esteem might prove the suspicion to be fact, this dysfunctional sense of self is often deeply hidden in the subconscious. As a result, low self-esteem is usually carried into adulthood.

This hidden sense of self is the source of most other kinds of personal dysfunction. Characteristics such as arrogance, perfectionism, procrastination, people-pleasing, control and manipulation, passive-aggressive behavior, and self-sabotage are some of the ways adults try to cope with low self-esteem. They go about seeking relief from their pain in the form of outside validation. At best, this kind of remedy is only temporary. In the long run it actually reinforces one's feelings of unworthiness and fails to address the true cause of that belief.

Overcoming this condition requires deep personal change in the sense of self. Through the transformation process, the emerging Christ sense transcends low self-esteem. This is a change in which one's worthiness is no longer questionable or dependent on others.

Emotional Dishonesty

People with this condition believe that emotions such as anger, fear, sadness, or confusion are unacceptable and must be bottled up for fear of losing control, being criticized, rejected, abandoned, or becoming vulnerable to ridicule, punishment or exploitation. Because of this condition, they cannot enter into honest and truly intimate relationships.

Relationship Dishonesty

This characteristic is based on the belief that one's self-interest is likely to conflict with the self-interest of others. People with this condition imagine that hiding their ego-based self-interest in relationships will give them an advantage in getting what they want.

This kind of dishonesty usually gets revealed, and distrust becomes an increasing factor in the relationship. Practicing relationship dishonesty actually nurtures the false belief that conflicting self-interest is the ultimate truth about human interactions. Most of the characteristics that make up a damaged ego involve some form of relationship dishonesty.

Manipulation of Emotions

Controlling and manipulating the feelings and reactions of others is the ego's attempt to overcome perceived threats and get what it wants. People with this characteristic believe that only by controlling others' emotions are they protected against the possibility of criticism, rejection, abandonment, ridicule, or punishment.

Control and Dominance

This characteristic is usually acquired through developmental experiences with adults who used it as a life strategy. The ego sense of self, through control and dominance of life circumstances and the actions of others, seeks to ensure its self-interest and reduce the possibility of harm. Often this involves emotional, physical, or financial threats to other people's security and sense of well-being if they do not behave as directed.

People with this characteristic tend to be attracted to individuals with low self-esteem who are looking for someone to become dependant on. The cost of this condition is relationships devoid of any real love or trust, given or received.

Abdicating Responsibility

This characteristic is usually established during developmental years, acquired through relationships with people who try to exercise excessive levels of control over children as they mature. Youths subjected to such treatment fail to develop confidence in making decisions and either reluctantly or willingly yield this responsibility to the adults. Children have little choice in the matter, considering that controlling adults hold unquestionable power over them. Unfortunately, this is usually carried into adulthood, where it creates great conflict.

People with this condition want to be in charge of their own destiny but lack the confidence to make decisions. This characteristic is always accompanied by low self-esteem, further exacerbating the threat of making a mistake. The payoff is that any negative experiences in life can be blamed on others. Seeing others as the perpetrators, the victim's sense of moral superiority provides temporary relief from low self-esteem.

People-Pleasing

This is a strategy in which individuals attempt to alter their sense of self for the purpose of gaining a desired response from others. Often this characteristic has been so pervasive that the individual never developed a true sense of self. Exhausting and very unfulfilling, people-pleasing usually results in failed relationships. Yet because it is an ingrained strategy, the people-pleaser will find another person and start the remaking of self all over again.

Because of the efforts and energy needed to conform to whatever they believe others want, people with this condition often become resentful. Convinced that the other person is demanding the change, thus abdicating their personal responsibility, the resentment grows. Individuals who are prone to this condition frequently find themselves in relationships with controlling personalities who exploit this willingness to give up their identity.

Dependency on Others

People with this characteristic suffer from low self-esteem and severe lack of confidence, making them financially, emotionally, socially, or physically dependent on others. They believe someone else can and will make their lives good. This form of faulty dependency conflicts with the true self, so it never satisfies. Resentment occurs when others fail to provide what the individual is counting on. Continued responses to life from this perspective strengthen feelings of low self-esteem. The evolutionary emergence of the Christ sense of self is the solution.

Depression and Self-Pity

This characteristic has its origins in a history of dysfunctional and less-than-satisfactory life experiences. It is based on a belief that the current ego-based sense of self is the only possibility; therefore, the future holds no promise, only more of what has happened in the past. The payoff for people with this condition is release from the risk and responsibility of trying to create a meaningful life. Sometimes depressed people blame others, sometimes themselves.

Anxiety

This deep-seated, free-floating kind of nonspecific fear results from an ego sense of self that relies on outer circumstances for quality of life. People thus afflicted know they cannot control even a few of those circumstances, and this realization makes them more and more anxious. There's a payoff in the early stages, when they still believe in the rewards that might come from successful control.

Perfectionism

This characteristic is based on the fantasy that it is possible to get everything right and that, with perfection, life will be satisfying. Perfectionism is usually acquired in the developmental stages of life, the result of trying to please others who have high expectations and little tolerance for mistakes. The payoff is the illusion that the ego is capable of perfection and should or will achieve it.

Perfectionists may appear arrogant in holding themselves to a much higher standard than others. As perfection proves unachievable, however, people with this condition may quit trying to achieve altogether and even sabotage their own efforts. This is purposely done to avoid the potential disappointment of failing to be perfect. *"I can't live up to my own standards, so why try?"*

Depression and self-pity can set in. Again, the answer is not in repairing the ego but in transcending it through the emerging divine sense of self that knows all efforts are worthy and serve to bring meaning and satisfaction into life. So-called mistakes are important in living and are valued learning experiences

Sexual Dysfunction

The sexual instinct in human beings is often as strong as our instinct for survival. Thus, all characteristics of a damaged ego can express themselves in a person's sexuality. It shouldn't be surprising that people with a damaged ego use sex as a way to cope with or compensate for deep, hidden feelings of low self-esteem.

People afflicted with this condition seek positive (or, in some cases, negative) sexual attention in an attempt to prove themselves attractive, desirable, and worthy. They may attempt to find sexual partners and situations that give them the illusion of control and power. Rape, pedophilia, prostitution, and extramarital affairs are extreme examples of these approaches to sexuality.

Paradoxically, intimate encounters can add to a person's feelings of low self-esteem even while being self-gratifying. Because of this, sexual activity can become addictive. Sexual addiction develops much like other addictions. All addicts seek a drug or experience that provides short-term gratification at the expense of long-term quality of life. This results in continued low self-esteem, a feeling that the addict keeps trying to get relief from through a repetition of unsuccessful behaviors.

For individuals who associate sexual feelings and activities with shame and guilt, the ability to enter into and maintain intimate sexual relationships may be severally hampered. In this case, sexual fantasy and masturbation can become the addiction as the ego shies away from relationships that might bring feelings of failure or inadequacy.

The cost to sexually dysfunctional people is the absence of a true partnership that is physical, emotional, and spiritual. As in most of the other characteristics of a damaged ego, repair is not a satisfactory solution. The emerging Christ sense of self is.

The examples above are some of the more typical ego characteristics that are discovered in the life review process. There are many other ways that self-centered fears are expressed in people's lives and relationships. An honest inventory taken from the perspective of the first three steps will disclose the ones each of us has inherited.

Now we will look to the renunciation faculty of mind as the next step in the process of transcending and transforming these pain-inducing beliefs.

The power of renunciation, also known as elimination or release, is something we use all the time. It is easiest to see at the physical level. The body regularly disposes of those elements of food and water it no longer needs. Taking in nourishment and disposing of waste is one of the unique components that differentiate biological life from other chemical processes.

In Step Six we come into a new understanding of this principle of life as it applies to the activity of our minds. We begin to understand its application to our spiritual evolution, the transformation process leading us to Christ consciousness.

First, though, let's consider how we currently use this power in our daily mental and emotional lives. Here's a simple, everyday example of how renunciation refocuses the mind's activity. When hungry, you begin to focus on food—physically, emotionally, and mentally acknowledging that need. Then you determine what you want to eat, determine the best way to get it, and take action. Afterward, no longer hungry, you release your mind's focus on eating in order to make it available for the next activity.

This is a natural process and usually very easy. But say there is some sort of problem, such as slow service at a restaurant. Irritated, you might find yourself in a state of mind that doesn't allow you to fully focus on other things. Dwelling on this irksome situation, you use up creative mind energy in feeling resentful and trying to place blame. The same could be true if the food wasn't to your liking or you felt uncomfortable with your dining partners. Any number of things that are judged "bad" can cause an emotional state that will adversely affect the ease with which you release the last activity of the mind in order to focus on what's next.

Experiences that are judged exceptionally "good" also can be difficult to release, particularly if they seem to provide an unparalleled degree of satisfaction. Examples include bingeing on sweets and other types of overindulging. In this case eating provides a high level of emotional or physical pleasure that isn't present when the mind is focused on the regular activities of life. This attachment to food impairs the ability of the mind to release its focus.

When your mind takes the middle ground—accepting an experience as is and judging it reasonably satisfactory—it is usually easy to release your attention and move on. A key factor here is judgment—judgment of the experience. The more the experience is deemed satisfactory, the easier it can be released.

Because we have judged some of our past experiences as bad, we have become attached to them. Our objective in this transformation process is to find good in our lives and to know that all experiences— past, present, and future—serve our evolution toward Christhood. Therefore, they all have good within them.

There are striking examples of how the principle of renunciation has been expressed in the evolution of life on our planet. Consider eyesight and flight. Scientists believe eyesight developed independently in 20 to 60 species at about the same time. Now, millions of species are genetically programmed for eyesight. With this adaptation in place, evolutionary creative energy is released and available for other adaptations. In birds, the creative energy of evolution is no longer focused on the development of flight as an adaptation. Birds, many insects, and a few mammals are now genetically programmed to grow wings and fly.

In the case of primates, changes in evolutionary focus can be seen in the way body shapes, nervous systems, and brains have evolved. These physiological changes brought about increased self-awareness, competitive behavior, social structures, importance of relationships, creative intelligence, and greater capacities for communication and development of culture. All of these are important, prerequisite characteristics for the emergence of a species whose members can become God-conscious—Christs!

So how is that important to our own evolutionary process, which is spiritual rather than biological or genetic in nature? Through the previous steps, we have come into a new realization of ourselves and our relationship to God and creation. We have begun to understand our nature as evolving primates sharing the same drive to satisfy instincts that are common to other primates and all life. We have begun to see that fears relating to survival, status, and reproduction have been prime motivations for the focus of our creative energy.

With greater understanding about the way life has evolved and the importance competition has played, it's easy to see how the use of power in the pursuit of self-interest (often at others' expense) seems to play such an important role in human nature. Cooperation played an essential part, too, but competition was particularly crucial in the earlier stages of our species' development. As part of our early evolution, we were designed to be in competitive conflict with one another and it's still true of the animal world.

In *Non-Zero, the Logic of Human Destiny*, Robert Wright describes how life responds to conflict and competition by creating more ways to cooperate. Cooperation motivated by a desire to transcend and eliminate conflict is one of the cornerstones of evolution. Certainly an increased capacity for finding peace in our lives motivates us to transcend the pain and suffering that come from conflict. Thus, the principle revealed in Wright's book underlies our personal motivation toward the evolution of our sense of self.

Many studies have documented that competition for survival and status is a primate characteristic, and humans have it in abundance. The instinct for survival, the need to be secure in the environment in order to live a full life, the need to be a valued member of society, and the need to experience worthiness will always be important aspects of human nature. Of course, eyesight is just as important—but how much energy do you devote to creating that capacity? The answer, of course, is none. The life force that we are has "renounced, released, and eliminated" the development of eyesight as a focus of our creative life energy. It now comes to us without conscious effort—like a gift.

We can easily accept this, but how many people believe that our old laundry list of primate instincts can be satisfied with as little struggle? Not many; most of us worry about those things. We worry about having enough money or about finding and keeping an intimate, committed relationship.

Jesus advocated, however, that we no longer apply fear-based creative energy to these aspects of life. He advocated a conscious awareness of our relationship with God in which these elements come to us as easily as we acquire eyesight.

"Therefore do not worry, saying, 'What will we eat?' or 'What will we drink?' or 'What will we wear?' For it is the Gentiles who strive for all these things; and indeed your heavenly Father knows that you need all these things. But strive first for the kingdom of God and his righteousness, and all these things will be given to you as well." (Matthew 6:31)

Don't worry? It will be given to you? Whoa. What a radical change in human behavior that would be!

As human beings, we have become unique. We are radically different from even our closest relatives, the chimps. A major part of that uniqueness is our emerging divine nature.

This uniqueness is expressed in feelings of discontent whenever our mind energy remains focused on instinct satisfaction. In that condition we ultimately find something missing in life; in fact, when this becomes the entire focus of our minds, we inevitably experience suffering.

The source of this misery lies in doggedly believing that we will get all the happiness, meaning, or security we want and need by concentrating the mind's energy on instinct satisfaction. That was an earlier reality that served primate evolution, but it now needs to be released, eliminated, and renounced.

Though some forms of life seem to have completed their evolution, we humans are very definitely a work in progress. Thus, the more we resist our evolution into divine human beings and refuse to take our focus off instinct satisfaction, the more pain and suffering we create for ourselves and others.

The new understanding of our own personal struggles, gained through Steps Four and Five, helps us see the need for refocusing. And when the pain of resistance is finally relieved by love, faith, new understanding, and emerging wisdom, we find ourselves opening to something different. We become ready for Step Six, the use of our mind faculty of renunciation.

Before going into what things we will renounce and how we will do it, let's look at ourselves from one more perspective, that of traditional Christianity.

Traditional Christianity lays the blame for human suffering at the door of "sin" and calls for renunciation, elimination, and redemption. In truth, there is a great deal of merit in Christianity's attempt to identify aspects of our nature that no longer work—namely the so-called "seven deadly sins" of pride, greed, lust, envy, sloth, anger, and gluttony.

These aspects of human nature have not changed much over time, and part of the reason is that they have been judged "bad"—a judgment obviously not predicated on an understanding of evolution and the beneficial roles these characteristics played in earlier stages. As we have seen, it is difficult—if not impossible—to renounce, release, and refocus when the immediate prior experience is judged "bad" and when a state of unresolved conflict exists with these ways of being. As a result, self-condemnation based on traditional Christianity's concept of sin actually restricts our evolutionary change.

The "sins" of pride and its counterpart, envy, are good examples.

Pride is the characteristic of self-satisfaction and elevated self-esteem that comes from higher status in comparison to others in society. Highly prized in the world of competition, it often is the result of inherited traits and abilities and/or cultural advantages acquired through fortunate birth circumstances. It may also be manifested in a person's superior physical or mental capability to overcome adverse conditions.

Pride isn't solely a human trait. You can almost sense the satisfaction a well-bred dog feels as it prances around a show ring. Or watch how a highly pedigreed thoroughbred trots. In the wild, particularly among primates, you can see the difference in the comportment of the strongest and highest ranked individuals.

This comportment, this pride, marks these individuals as the best of the species. Being the best they usually have greatest access to the basics required for survival. Males get most of the breeding rights. Females usually get first access to food and have access to the best males for breeding, which additionally gives them the greatest chance of producing and successfully rearing quality offspring.

Envy is the other side of the coin. It is the desire in lower-ranked individuals to enjoy the benefits that seem to come from being recognized as superior, and it motivates them to raise themselves using any means possible. With success comes a greater chance for survival and possibly a higher place in the social and mating structure. Envy may not exist in some of the lower animals, but there is much evidence of it in most primates and certainly in human beings.

Pride and envy have both served evolution by increasing the chances of successful reproduction for the fittest individuals. Pride, in particular, is a good characteristic because it contributes to the reproduction of high-quality genetic material, thus increasing the quality of offspring and the species. Who doesn't want to marry a truly high-quality individual?

We value and reward people who demonstrate certain characteristics considered good or attractive. Consider the fame and fortune of top athletes, performers, politicians, and entrepreneurs, and also about what that means in terms of their sexual attractiveness. It is part of our human makeup to want to be recognized as valued, highly capable, attractive individuals. Many people pursue this experience as the ultimate in human satisfaction.

Other aspects of human nature that cause suffering can be seen in the same light. Greed arises from an instinct for securing abundant access to things needed to survive in a competitive and threatening world. Gluttony can be seen as the survival mechanism of storing energy for times of famine and lack. Sloth can be viewed as the inclination to reserve energy for a time when a great amount may be required. Anger may be seen as the energizing response to situations that threaten status, survival, or reproductive possibilities.

As we have found through personal experiences, these instinctual satisfactions, though once the focus of life energy, no longer provide us with the level of meaning and fulfillment we desire. We are now evolutionarily destined to find satisfaction and meaning through a new, spiritually awake mind in which we function from a state of conscious, creative union with God and all creation.

Our relationships will be measured according to a new standard— characterized by cooperation instead of competition and conflict driven by ego-based self-interest. Win/win responses to the ongoing stories of our lives will become the focus, replacing the win/lose mentality present in most competitive relationships.

Our instinctual needs for security, for an important and valued place in society, and for reproduction will still exist. But they will be met through intuitive guidance leading to expanded connections of mutual enhancement with other human beings and other life on Earth. Like eyesight, instinct satisfaction will no longer be the focus of our mental and physical creative energy. Instead, the focus will be on recognition and expression of our own and others' unique divine identities. Our needs will be satisfied naturally as a result of the full expression of our divine creative nature.

The move forward calls for a refocusing of mental energy, built on a proper understanding and illuminating use of the mind faculty of renunciation. The Sixth Step is our willingness to renounce instinct satisfaction in its many forms as the primary focus of mental energy. We will refocus not by judging ourselves bad because we may be proud, lustful, greedy, angry, slothful, envious, or gluttonous, but by judging these characteristics as no longer right for us.

We are destined for greater things, and we need to use our power of renunciation in order to move on. Like a baby who may feel unhappy and insecure when being weaned from an exclusive milk diet, we may resist the process. But through the change, the baby awakens to new kinds of nourishment in an unlimited world of tastes and foods. That is the same for us. Like the weaned infant, change is essential for our future well-being.

Our capacity for exercising renunciation is greatly enhanced when we can identify our own personal characteristics, the focus of our mind energy that needs to be changed. That's exactly what we've done with the fourth and fifth steps.

This is an extraordinary moment in the history of life on Earth. A species is actively and consciously participating in its own evolution! This has never happened before, but that's nothing to be concerned about. After all, the evolution of eyesight and flight was also unprecedented at one time. It appears that unprecedented evolutionary changes are actually quite normal.

The actual power—the will—to make change is the next faculty of mind in the transformation process. It is essential that we focus on the presence of a divine power, because at this stage of our evolution we don't possess the power to change our natures independently.

We must come to grips with that truth. We will need a new understanding of humility, a state of mind that allows the ego to be transformed. Humility will be needed because our continued transformation requires the divine Christ expression of will rather than the ego expression of will to accomplish the change.

It's the exercise of the mind faculty of renunciation from a place of newfound wisdom that opens us to the presence of God's will within us. In Step Seven we will tap the power that can actually transform human nature—our own and that of the human race.

Chapter Seven

WILL

In **Step Seven**, *we humbly ask God to remove our shortcomings.*

H aving accepted that growth, change, and evolution are unavoidable consequences of the human experience and having identified some of the ideas, beliefs, and attitudes that no longer serve us, we now are faced with the question of how to bring about the needed changes.

> *Will is the executive, resolving faculty of mind. The will moves to action all the other faculties of mind.* **Matthew is the apostle.**

Willingness is needed, naturally, and so is willpower. Willpower, consciously combined with creativity, is one of the hallmark characteristics that make human beings unique. In this step, we will learn how the limited expression of the mind faculty of will (as expressed in the ego) differs from that of God's power of will (as expressed in our emerging Christ nature).

With Step Seven, we resolve to take specific actions that will result in actual changes in our human nature. We will be considering a vastly different role of the will in accomplishing this goal, a role that stands in contrast to that which is considered normal in the affairs of humans.

Changing human nature is no small chore. So far, it has never been permanently accomplished through an act of human will. Political efforts intended to correct social ills have had some limited success in suppressing and controlling the negative qualities of human nature, but the nature itself remained pretty much unchanged. While religion has had a positive effect on humanity, it hasn't changed human nature much either.

One can find the entire spectrum of human nature, from the most loving aspects to the most terrifying, within the history of virtually every religious movement. Most of these religious movements, at their core, have been authentic and sincere efforts to alleviate the suffering of humanity, to find some sort of salvation for the human condition. At the same time, these very movements, Christianity included, have also demonstrated the worst in human nature.

On a personal level, changing human nature seems exceptionally difficult. Anyone who has made a serious attempt at personal growth knows how hard it is to change thought patterns and actions. Considering all that, you might wonder just how we are going to change our nature if the best efforts of individuals and the greatest minds and the greatest saints have not done so yet.

Part of the answer can be found in the human approach to problem solving. Another part can be found in past and current understandings of our relationship to God.

Let's deal with concepts about God first. Problems exist in the erroneous religious belief that God is a being or power separate from creation. This idea is still well entrenched in the consciousness of most people, though thankfully we are slowly growing away from it.

According to this belief, God is an absentee power who leaves us with the job of actually changing human nature—and the consequences of messing up. He observes and occasionally intervenes when the job is heading for sure failure. That particular kind of belief is inherent in most of the Old Testament, with a few exceptions where individuals had a heightened mystical experience of God.

Belief in an absent or distant God who observes, judges, rewards, and punishes has resulted in human beings feeling totally responsible for changing the state of the human condition. It's no secret, of course, that human nature needs to be transformed. Things we read in the newspaper and see on television every day confirm this, as does our own experiences.

And so we try the best we can, and we do have some limited success. Suffering has been significantly reduced and physical life extended. In many cases religious, spiritual, and even some political beliefs and practices have had an effect on reducing misery. Still, children die needlessly, people go hungry, lethal force is used as the bottom-line solution to human problems, and everybody eventually dies of something, whether from disease, accident, or bodily dysfunction.

Though religion has contributed meaningfully to many people's lives, the overall amount of cruelty in the world continues at a rate that should be unacceptable to us. Global communications have reduced the inclination to wholesale violations of human rights because the perpetrators and their abuses now get world attention. This has a positive effect because it exposes and inhibits some kinds of behaviors. Even so, it has little effect on changing motives.

Part of the reason humanity finds it so difficult to solve the problem of human nature is our predisposition to treat struggle as an accepted and dominant approach to life. This inherited instinct has been important in the evolution of life, but it now ties humans to the limitations of the physical world and the five senses, restricting our emerging capacity to tap into the divine level of creative power.

We certainly seem to love struggle, particularly the rewards attached to it. Struggling to the top of the corporate ladder pays well and provides power and prestige. Struggling to win athletic competitions has obvious payoffs. And aren't many of our greatest stories based on struggles and victories? Literary tragedies glorify the human capacity to never say die and to try, try, try again.

Struggle, in fact, is basic to most people in the world as we seek to earn a living, attract and keep a good mate, and raise children successfully. The point here is to understand how struggle—the use of the will—has served us and has been the natural and obvious way to approach problems and challenges. This inclination isn't something that's wrong with us; it's a major factor in our evolution and, as with most things, is inherently good.

However, it is most important now to see what Jesus pointed out—that the struggling use of the human will has lost some of its usefulness to us. It is no more useful for entering into Christ consciousness than is the ability to crawl on all fours useful to a 100-meter track star. In truth, when it is relied upon, it is a definite liability.

Jesus referred to the need to give up struggle in Matthew, Chapter 5. *"But I say to you, do not resist an evildoer. But if anyone strikes you on the right cheek, turn the other also; and if anyone wants to sue you and take your coat, give your cloak as well; and if anyone forces you to go one mile, go also the second mile."*

Radical idea, that—**not** struggling against evil. It might even sound impossible, though of course so might the Kingdom of Heaven! Yet this is God's promise to us. Jesus is saying that using the human will in continued struggles with the world, even with the so-called evil components of it, does not serve the purpose of bringing one into the promised kingdom. Victory cannot be obtained in the same old way through the workings of the ego, even when done in the name of God.

So He said to them, "You are those who justify yourselves in the sight of others; but God knows your hearts; for what is prized by human beings is an abomination in the sight of God." (Luke 16:15)

The use of tools in the struggle to solve problems is a wonderful human/primate characteristic and certainly a creative way to extend and amplify the will. The idea of using tools has even been extended to the realm of religion.

Various religious practices seem to qualify as tools in accomplishing the religious life. Prayer, meditation, various rituals, sacraments, ceremonies, and many other practices and disciplines have emerged throughout world religions, all with the purpose of assisting human beings in attaining a religious or spiritual goal that would somehow answer the problem of human suffering and death.

As with all tools, using these is an act of will. It is an act of will when a monk takes a vow of silence. It is an act of will to pray. It is an act of will to fast or take a vow of poverty or chastity. It is an act of will to purposefully use prayer to deny the power of some negative condition, and it is an act of will to steadfastly affirm the positive.

The use of physical, mental, spiritual, and religious tools are undeniable elements of human nature and have served us well up to this time. They will continue to do that, but will never be the complete answer.

A good analogy is how a house gets built. You can have all the hammers, saws, nails and lumber you need, but without an understanding of the principles of construction you won't get very far. In actuality, you will probably get very frustrated. Purchasing new or better tools won't make any difference. They can't replace solid knowledge.

Consciousness reconstruction—the creation of a new mind in the human being—is much the same way. Without the right understanding of the principles of spiritual evolution, which Jesus and a few others taught and demonstrated, there is little hope of experiencing transformation by simply using or changing spiritual tools, no matter how practiced or willful one gets at using them.

Learning a new way to use the will without struggling is an essential part of the process of transformation. Now we get into the question of how to use it that way.

Up to this point, the struggle to be best has been part of life's makeup, and we still love and value it because of the way it has served life. That is good, but at the same time it's important to realize that the possibility of failure is inherent in struggle. Members of our species are not made equal, at least at the biological or physical level. We can't all be Michael Jordans or Albert Einsteins, no matter how much we practice or study.

This inequality motivates the struggle to achieve superiority. By excelling or at least being adequate, we establish our position in society. Nobody wants to fail, and the fear of it happening often becomes a major cause of stress, even if unstated or just subconsciously experienced. It is this belief that must be removed in the spiritually transformed mind.

In Jesus' mind, there was never a possibility of failure. His will and the will of God were identical and instantly assured. When the possibility of failure is gone—**God doesn't fail**—what need is there for struggle?

The possibility of failure does not exist in the consciousness of Christ—in the human mind that is consciously in union with God. In the transformation process, faith begins to replace the ego-based human willpower approach to life. The story of Jesus and Peter walking on water illustrates how the fear of failure and struggle lose their usefulness as we evolve.

And early in the morning He came walking toward them on the sea. But when the disciples saw Him walking on the sea, they were terrified, saying, "It is a ghost!" And they cried out in fear. But immediately Jesus spoke to them and said, "Take heart, it is I; do not be afraid." Peter answered him, "Lord, if it is you, command me to come to you on the water." He said, "Come." So Peter got out of the boat, started walking on the water, and came toward Jesus. But when he noticed the strong wind, he became frightened and, beginning to sink, he cried out, "Lord, save me!" Jesus immediately reached out his hand and caught him, saying to him, "You of little faith, why did you doubt?" (Matthew 14:25-31)

This story points out clearly what a liability our human inclination for struggle becomes as we move toward evolving into Christ consciousness. Yet, who can stop struggling? It's as much a part of our nature as walking upright!

In evolution all life forms are under the overall will of God. Our primate ancestors did not grow opposable thumbs through acts of conscious will. It was part of a pattern of evolutionary response as our species moved toward self-consciousness and eventual awareness of its divine nature. Like all previous steps of evolution, this next one will also be an act of God's will.

Having become self-conscious, we humans must consciously volunteer for and cooperate with the process. As part of this cooperation, we are asked to give up struggling and no longer base our actions on fear of failure or pride of success. As you will recall, we surrendered the circumstances of our lives in Steps One, Two, and Three. Through that, we discovered a new understanding about the presence and power of God.

In Step Seven, we surrender the transformation process. We do so because of our seemingly insatiable, genetically programmed appetite to struggle in the world and our understanding that, at this point in our evolution, we cannot transform ourselves. We humbly ask God to do it for us.

We need to be weaned from our appetite for struggle in order to be fed directly from the mind energy of God—to know our union with the creative forces of the universe, with the eternal and unfailing presence of love. Weaned from our appetites for instinct satisfaction as the food of life, we would now feed on the food of God as Jesus did.

But he said to them, "I have food to eat that you do not know about." So the disciples said to one another, "Surely no one has brought him something to eat?" Jesus said to them, "My food is to do the will of him who sent me and to complete his work. Do you not say, 'Four months more, then comes the harvest'? But I tell you, look around you, and see how the fields are ripe for harvesting. The reaper is already receiving wages and is gathering fruit for eternal life, so that sower and reaper may rejoice together." (John, Chapter 32)

For many, this step is somewhat disconcerting. Everyone is ready and willing to give up the pain and possible failure inherent in the world of struggle. At the same time, they may find it much harder to give up the possibilities of rewards that result from it. Those personal ego-based victories are our greatest temptations.

God's promise is that experiencing the kingdom Jesus demonstrated will be far more satisfying than anything brought about by demonstrations of adequacy, superiority, or successful struggle in the world. There is no possibility of failure!

Then Peter said in reply, "Look, we have left everything and followed you. [Peter and the disciples had given up their livelihoods.] *What then will we have?" Jesus said to them, "Truly I tell you, at the renewal of all things, when the Son of Man* [anyone who has evolved into the Christ nature] *is seated on the throne of his glory, you who have followed me will also sit on twelve thrones, judging the twelve tribes of Israel* [the twelve faculties of mind]. *And everyone who has left houses or brothers or sisters or father or mother or children or fields, for my name's sake, will receive a hundredfold, and will inherit eternal life."* (Matthew 19:27-29)

Being weaned doesn't mean we will no longer eat actual food, reproduce, or enjoy and benefit from the society of others. It just means that our efforts and rewards will no longer come through a struggle to obtain these things. They will now come through our union with the creative mind of God.

When we ask, God will wean us. And we will be free to create from the love of creating, rather than from the fear of failure.

At first it may seem we are losing something, that we're being denied the satisfaction of obtaining all the things we crave, like worldly security, prestige, power, and sex. In reality we are gaining the opportunity to surrender our human inclination to struggle. Like oil and water, the Kingdom of Heaven and humankind's inclination for struggle do not mix.

As we surrender, giving up the "milk" of the world, we gradually receive the food of God in replacement. And like an infant discovering solid food, we slowly wake up to a new world of spiritual nourishment beyond anything imagined.

Jesus knew what he was talking about in referring to God as a loving parent. To be gently weaned, even when we fuss and complain, and to be fed and nourished in amounts that are just right for our growth is the truest evidence of this.

Jesus said that we are the children of God. When we know who we are, when we know we are inherently good and loved, and when we know we are designed to spiritually mature in an orderly process of growth, then we will not be afraid to ask God and we will be transformed. God's will is to do exactly that for us. And through that process God's will and ours will come into conscious unity in the time and manner that's right for each of us.

First, though, it will require us to humbly rely on God to bring us the circumstances of life that will further our transformation. This prayer—which I modified from the book *Alcoholics Anonymous*—exemplifies the kind of commitment to humility that this step requires.

> *God, I am willing that you should have all of me.*
> *I pray that You now remove from me every single*
> *aspect of my character that no longer serves*
> *my usefulness to You, my fellows and*
> *my transformation into Christhood.*
> *May Your will be done always.*

Chapter Eight

ORDER

*In **Step Eight**, we make a list of all persons we have harmed and become willing to make amends to them all.*

The practice of forgiveness is one of the essential requirements of the transformation process. It brings God's presence and God's will for expanding love into relationships that have been previously characterized by fear-based struggle and conflict.

> *Order is the faculty of mind in which harmony, balance, right adjustment, and evolutionary progress are brought about through a sequence of action and events.*
> **James, son of Alpheaus, isthe apostle.**

In the next two steps, we apply the newfound wisdom and understanding that come from our emerging divine nature in order to bring forgiveness to past and present experiences. As we take responsibility for being God's instrument of new peace, our consciousness is permanently changed. Opening our lives and ourselves to the influence of this emerging Christ nature, we begin to transcend the law of cause and effect.

Jesus addressed the law of cause and effect in his teachings. In Matthew 5:25-26: *"Come to terms quickly with your accuser while you are on the way to court with him or your accuser may hand you over to the judge, and the judge to the guard, and you will be thrown into prison. Truly I tell you, you will never get out until you have paid the last penny."*

Also in Matthew 7:2-5: *"For with the judgment you make you will be judged, and the measure you give will be the measure you get. Why do you see the speck in your neighbor's eye, but do not notice the log in your own eye? Or how can you say to your neighbor, 'Let me take the speck out of your eye,' while the log is in your own eye? You hypocrite, first take the log out of your own eye and then you will see clearly to take the speck out of your neighbor's eye."*

One of Jesus' most profound teachings about this divine evolutionary journey came as a response to the disciples' request for him to teach them how to pray. In the Lord's Prayer he affirmed a new order of life and offered an orderly way in which his disciples could turn their minds toward God and the transformation process. Forgiveness is an essential part of the prayer and the establishment of this new order.

We will be looking at some of the prayer's components as we consider the mind faculty of order. First, however, let's take a look at the language—its true meaning and purpose.

The wording reflects the common worldview of its time, when God was seen as separate and distant and the culture was patriarchal. In order for his ideas to be understood, Jesus used language consistent with the culture. Today, with culture moving away from that patriarchal nature, some people would reject the prayer. But like much of the Bible, it simply needs reinterpreting in order to find its more profound level of spiritual truth.

It's this level of truth that transcends temporary cultural and social influences. And it is evident from Jesus' opening statement.

"Our Father, who art in Heaven"

With these words, Jesus makes it clear that we are children of God. Heaven is the spiritual realm of God in which we can know ourselves that way.

"Hallowed be thy name."

In the culture of Jesus' day, names were used to identify something or someone's nature. Thus, God's nature as spirit and truth is hallowed, meaning it is of the highest importance and value. Because we are children of God, our essential nature is also spiritual, and our essence has its source in the same truth that is the nature of God.

The relationship with our creator is far more sacred than any other, including those with our earthly parents. We help establish this as a reality for ourselves by consciously moving our focus from the physical to the spiritual. This recognition of our true nature as spiritual heirs of God will become our own reality in the transformation process. Jesus knew it was essential to begin affirming this truth. The true purpose of his prayer is to alter our own consciousness, not to elicit a response from a distant and separate God.

"Thy kingdom come, thy will be done, on earth as it is in heaven."

Again, this is a statement of truth, not a request. In it Jesus is consciously affirming that the emerging Kingdom of God on Earth is coming. He is saying it is God's will for human beings to experience the creative power of divine love and the eternal nature of life while physically alive.

This unprecedented state of consciousness is an evolutionary step. It previously existed only in the realm of pure spirit. Jesus, who had come into this state, expressed this new reality and spiritual authority in the miraculous ways he affected the lives of people around him. In this prayer he is instructing disciples to affirm this condition of mind as their future and as the ultimate future of a transformed humanity.

"Give us this day our daily bread."

People often think of this as a request for actual food. But it refers instead to a focus on God's will as all we need to thrive. True food is to be in union with the will of God. In that condition of mind, all else will be provided, including an abundant supply of the essentials for physical life. Other examples in the Bible, such as the miracles of the loaves and fishes, teach and demonstrate this same truth.

"And forgive us our debts, as we also have forgiven our debtors."

In this statement Jesus addresses the need for forgiveness in order to detach from the negative and fear-based beliefs that control much of our lives. He is saying we cannot experience complete forgiveness of ourselves unless we forgive others. The two are tied together at the spiritual level, and achieving complete forgiveness is an essential part of divine evolution.

As discussed earlier, the nature of Christ consciousness is access to a great creative power, to be used according to the personal will and needs of the individual who has it. Because unconditional love and unforgiveness cannot coexist in the same mind, that power is available to people only to the degree that they have taken this step.

In Jesus' last moments on the cross, he affirmed complete forgiveness for all those who were responsible for his crucifixion. He did it so that all would hear and understand the importance of forgiveness.

When they came to the place that is called The Skull, they crucified Jesus there with the criminals, one on his right and one on his left. Then Jesus said, "Father, forgive them; for they do not know what they are doing." And they cast lots to divide his clothing. (Luke 23:33-34)

Jesus fully understood that his teachings posed a threat. The religious hierarchy headed by Herod supported certain privileged people in roles of authority and superiority. The people who maintained the hierarchy taught that this order of things was the will of God and that God had ordained severe punishment for any who opposed it.

The laws governing the Israelites were based on spiritual revelations, but the revelations had been filtered through and altered by the human ego. And because of the self-centered fears that exist in the human/primate consciousness, the religious order had deteriorated into a state of tyranny through the abuse of power.

Here was proof that the laws were far more a human expression of order than an eternal expression of divine order. Through this, it becomes apparent that the human tendency to make religious laws sacred and rigid hinders spiritual evolution and often brings suffering. Jesus' intention to challenge the established religious order brought about his own crucifixion.

Jesus was able to authentically forgive because he experienced himself eternally alive and knew his true nature could never be damaged, even by death. He also knew that those who felt threatened by his teachings simply didn't yet understand this truth. They were acting according to their limited understanding of the nature of life and their relationship to God. They were instinctively protecting their status and attempting to neutralize threats.

As discussed in earlier steps, competition and conflicting self-interests are hallmarks of the evolution of life. In all primate species, the establishment of order is essential for survival. In human beings, this instinct can be seen as the written and unwritten laws that set up hierarchies in families and nations, and it's something that's still very important to us.

The establishment of order serves two purposes in human society. First, it ensures the security of the social structure, encompassing not just individuals who have mutual self-interests but also those with conflicting or competing ones. Second, it ensures that individuals who excel are allowed to do so, as long as it doesn't threaten the social fabric.

In the free enterprise system of economics, this means that if I make a better, less expensive widget than you do, it's acceptable for me to go after your customers, even if this puts you out of business. At the same time, order dictates that I must compete within rules governing fairness. The same holds true for finding a mate. This tribal order establishes the framework by which we contend with one another in efforts to survive, adapt, and compete without destroying the fabric that holds society together.

Problems arise, however, because people who are the best at establishing themselves in society's higher positions often make the rules that secure them in those roles. In Jesus' day, the major ruling order in his society was religion-based.

Religious-based social and cultural structures are usually the result of attempts to live in conscious relationship with God. But Jesus recognized that the ruling hierarchy in his part of the world had deteriorated into an oppressive form intended to maintain power and privilege for a select few.

This is consistent with genetic and biological inclination for survival of the fittest, an essential characteristic in the evolution of primates. In human beings, this imperative has been transcended by the divine imperative for spiritual evolution into Christ consciousness. And this means change.

As should be obvious, a major part of this change needs to be in the way we use our mind faculty of order. The ego-based expression of this mind faculty is evident in the way we try to secure personal self-interests—in other words, to exercise some kind of control over people and circumstances. We can easily see it in the way we react to perceived threats to our physical well-being, our sexual and reproductive instinct, or our place of importance within society.

If possible, we try to establish order in our lives to neutralize actual or perceived threats. In most cases, we use the laws of our social system or the rules of social behavior to accomplish that. In other cases, we may use threats, manipulation, coercion, or even force.

The increasing role of competition and conflicting self-interests can be observed in children as they become teenagers. They often experience great stress around the need to be found attractive and desirable within the society of their peers. Competitive sports and other events provide many other examples of this state of mind.

These types of competition are nearly always based on the instinct to be judged superior through win/lose competition and conflict. The winners are rewarded; the losers are not. That is how hierarchies and status are established within the tribe. Politics, business, and even baby contests are based on the same idea.

The establishment of order is surely essential to our current level of evolution. Good rules and boundaries generate a healthy home environment for successful child rearing. Mutually accepted laws and political borders create order among disparate groups. This is as true for the family and its domain as it is for the nation and its international boundaries.

In a democratic society order is usually based on the principle of the inherent worth of all people. Though not always lived up to, this principle is there and it's an important early step toward the greater establishment of divine order. Through the emergence of the divine mind faculty of order, we are creating a future in which we will easily establish an order that does not require threats or punishment for its preservation.

Ultimately, divine order can be found deep within every situation and condition, even if it is sometimes hard for us to see it. In Steps Eight and Nine, we will discover the truth of our own histories. But before we do that, let's examine one more example of how this truth is expressed in nature.

In the history of organic life on Earth, scientists have discovered five major extinction events, each of which resulted in the loss of many or most species existing at the time. Life responded by expanding the creation of new forms, and evolution continued. In the same way, the crucifixion of Jesus did not result in his extinction as the eternal living Christ. This event actually facilitated the expansion of the movement he initiated.

In both examples, divine order ensured that life did not fail because of an extinction event. The very presence of that divine order—the activity of the Holy Spirit—is the force working within each of us, moving us toward evolutionary change in our lives today.

In Step Seven, we learned of the need to release our genetic predisposition to struggle as a means to entering the Kingdom of God. Like Jesus, we need to find a new way of responding to whatever seems to threaten us.

Threatening conditions have been present from the very beginning; some have been created by life itself. Single-cell organisms began during a time when the main component of Earth's atmosphere was carbon dioxide. These earliest life forms gave off oxygen as a waste product, polluting the very atmosphere in which they evolved. Divine order responded with the evolution of animal life, which thrived on this oxygen and gave off carbon dioxide as a waste product. Thus, plant life provided the conditions by which animal life could evolve and in turn was supported by it. Order prevailed in its will to create relationships of mutual enhancement.

A state of peace and harmony, the kind of order that is the nature of God's will of love, will allow us entry into Christ consciousness. An essential part of that process will be granting forgiveness in all areas of our lives where fear and struggle brought our relationships with others into disorder.

In Step Eight we look at our past and present relationships from a new perspective, informed by the emerging Christ in our nature. We may have experienced oppression or unfair treatment, particularly in childhood, perhaps harmed by the very people who should have given love and nurturing. For many, these circumstances seem to repeat themselves later in life; some of us even become perpetrators of the same kinds of conditions we were victims of as children. These experiences may strengthen attachments to the very beliefs that result in suffering or cause us to create defenses.

On review, we often find that these very defenses block us from creating relationships that are authentically mutually enhancing, primarily because of preexisting mistrust. At this stage, we begin to identify specific changes that are needed in the way we relate to others.

o We do this through a further **evaluation** of how our ego has expressed fears in past relationships, perhaps using therapy to gain greater understanding and compassion for those who seemed responsible for instilling fears in us.

o Even with this greater understanding, however, we need to both seek and grant **forgiveness**. Only in this way can we bring final resolution to past conflicts and become authentically detached from these fears. By looking at the past—not living in the past, as some would suggest—we finally become free of it.

o We will now ask ourselves **how we related** to others from the perspective of competition and conflict of self-interests, specifically looking for ways we harmed or diminished other people.

o We will **make a list** of everyone who experienced harm or a diminished sense of self through relationships with us.

o We will become willing to **change the outcome** by adding a chapter to those stories. This only comes through granting forgiveness and making amends. From a purely human perspective, it may appear that we were justified in securing our own self-interest in some situations. But from the perspective of divine order—where a greater reality of love and harmony now exists for us—we will need to look well past the level of appearances.

We are asked to look at relationships with the conviction that we will forgive or seek forgiveness from everyone we ever related to as an enemy of any kind—any relationship in which feelings of injustice, anger, fear, resentment, jealousy, and the like contributed to creating a negative experience. *"Love your enemies,"* Jesus said in Luke, Chapter 6. *"Do good to those who hate you, bless those who curse you, pray for those who abuse you."*

By adopting this attitude, it may at first appear we will become doormats for anyone to walk on. Jesus is saying, however, that there is a way into the Kingdom of God and that it requires forgiveness. We must come to know the truth that God's love exists in every condition of our lives, indeed of all people's lives. Waking up spiritually, we become increasingly aware of the satisfying and important role we are to play. Through the creative power of the Christ in us, we can play this role without struggle as we come to know the presence of God in our minds and hearts.

Our previous efforts to make life work through control were usually motivated by passionate desires to secure self-interest. This motivation must now be transformed into a passion for experiencing the divine presence of love and for the expression of abundant and eternal life through our conscious union with God.

Step Nine is where we begin to live lives that are in divine order, characterized by increased enthusiasm and passion as well as very real decreases in human conflict, struggle, and suffering. In the next chapter we will deal specifically with how the emerging Christ in each of us will accomplish that.

Chapter Nine

ZEAL

*In the **Ninth Step**, we make direct amends to people whenever possible, except when doing so would injure them or others.*

Though a new divine sense of self should be emerging at this point, the idea of directly approaching people for the purpose of achieving authentic forgiveness will surely seem difficult, if not impossible. Recognizing that most people feel resistance to this part of the transformation process, this chapter will address making amends from two different perspectives.

Zeal is the enthusiastic, passionate faculty of mind. **Simon is the apostle.**

First, we will demonstrate how absolutely essential this step is to the transformation process. Then, we will deal with specific ways of making amends in order to reduce the anxiety that our ego sense of self may be experiencing. In both approaches, we will discuss the role of the passion, or enthusiasm, faculty of mind.

Passion, enthusiasm, and zeal identify the faculty of mind that moves things beyond the ordinary and the mundane. Jesus was very passionate about his particular mission. So was Adolf Hitler. The word "extraordinary" can be easily applied to both of them, though they are examples of opposite ends of the spectrum of human nature.

In terms of evolution, Jesus was an extraordinary model of God's will for progression. On the other hand, Hitler was an extraordinary model of the fear-based tendency toward regression. Jesus talked about and demonstrated a new heaven on Earth. Hitler created a living hell.

Each demonstrated powerful use of the faculties of mind. The difference between them was internal motivation. One was love and unity; the other, fear and separation.

Passion, like all of the faculties of mind, can be applied in either regressive or progressive ways. When mind faculties are applied to life from the perspective of ego-based instinct satisfaction only, the condition is regressive and results in excessive suffering. Excessive (and unneeded) suffering is a very good definition of hell, and that was the obvious case in Hitler's creation of Nazism.

Let's consider Hitler from a primate point of view. The desire to be the "alpha male," the number one male in the tribe, is a primate instinct. In chimpanzees, our species' closest relatives, males attain and maintain alpha male status by dominating and/or gaining the loyalty of others.

There certainly seems to be a tendency toward that in humans, particularly among males. Growing up, I learned that one of the great things about living in the United States was that any boy could be president. This was presumed to be every American boy's dream. Political incorrectness aside, it demonstrates the alpha male instinct, although we human beings would likely assign higher motives to such ambitions.

From small social groups to large nations, there is the same kind of characteristic and drive toward attaining power or influence. Leaders attempt to gain number one status through force or intimidation. Others do so by developing alliances. Most use a combination.

The alpha instinct is a male quality among most primates. This could account for the fact that men are more often found in the highest leadership positions in competitive situations. It doesn't necessarily mean they are more qualified than females, but it may indicate a greater passion for attaining status. (There is also a strong "alpha female" instinct in which status, power, and influence are also very important, but it may express itself differently.)

In most of the primate species there is an alpha male, and nearly always this individual is characterized by high ambition, enthusiasm, and passion. Hitler had those traits and also exhibited tribalism, a primate characteristic that is called nationalism at the human level. The German dictator wanted to establish himself as the alpha male of a tribe composed of "superior" human beings. In so doing he attempted to identify and then either subdue or annihilate what he considered members of "inferior" tribes.

Researchers have observed chimpanzees exhibiting this same kind of violent behavior, in which males of one troop enlarge their territory by wiping out the males—and even less-desirable females—of neighboring troops. Human history is full of similar attempts to conquer and take over others' territory. From an earlier evolutionary perspective, the weaker tribes were fair game; survival of the fittest was the rule.

The Gospels indicate that Jesus went through a period of temptation before publicly expressing his Christ powers. One temptation specifically addressed the passion for status that is part of our human inheritance.

Then the devil led him up and showed him in an instant all the kingdoms of the world. And the devil said to him, "To you I will give their glory and all this authority; for it has been given over to me, and I give it to anyone I please. If you, then, will worship me, it will all be yours." Jesus answered him, "It is written, 'Worship the Lord your God, and serve only him.'" (Luke 4:5-8)

This temptation was based on the illusion—the lie—that Christ powers could be used to satisfy old primate-based instincts. Jesus knew better.

The "devil" in the passage above symbolizes the fear and illusion of separation that lie at the heart of the ego sense of self and the way individuals struggle with one another, especially the struggle to become number one. But the devil has no independent reality. It is no more than a shared state of consciousness in which many of us act from the same untruth.

Probably most primate researchers and evolutionary biologists would agree that alpha male and tribal instincts have allowed Earth's species to adapt and survive. Because of the human tendency to abuse power, however, they have often been considered among our species' gravest defects. But they might better be seen as simply our primate inheritance—not as human characteristics at all.

Nearly all human beings find the values and behaviors of people like Hitler and societies like the Nazis abhorrent. Most find the teachings of Jesus and other religious leaders and the values and principles of most religions as being more representative of how we would like to see ourselves as human beings.

Inherent in these two extremes are the characteristics of our past and future evolutionary states. The suffering—the hell—brought into the human experience by Hitler and others like him is the consequence of resistance to a divinely determined evolutionary future. The fact that there are consequences for resisting and regressing in evolution is certainly God's will; yet the activation of these consequences requires human initiative and effort. The movement forward to greater love also requires human cooperation. Thus, we are called to choose one or the other.

This truth is symbolically recognized very early in the story of Cain and Abel (Genesis 4:3-16).

In the course of time Cain brought to the Lord an offering of the fruit of the ground, and Abel for his part brought of the firstlings of his flock, their fat portions. And the Lord had regard for Abel and his offering but for Cain and his offering he had no regard. So Cain was very angry, and his countenance fell.

The Lord said to Cain, "Why are you angry, and why has your countenance fallen? If you do well, will you not be accepted? And if you do not do well, sin is lurking at the door; its desire is for you, but you must master it."

Cain said to his brother Abel, "Let us go out to the field." And when they were in the field, Cain rose up against his brother Abel and killed him. Then the Lord said to Cain, "Where is your brother Abel?" He said, "I do not know; am I my brother's keeper?"

And the Lord said, "What have you done? Listen, your brother's blood is crying out to me from the ground! And now you are cursed from the ground, which has opened its mouth to receive your brother's blood from your hand. When you till the ground, it will no longer yield to you its strength; you will be a fugitive and a wanderer on the earth."

Cain said to the Lord, "My punishment is greater than I can bear! Today you have driven me away from the soil, and I shall be hidden from your face; I shall be a fugitive and a wanderer on the earth, and anyone who meets me may kill me."

Then the Lord said to him, "Not so! Whoever kills Cain will suffer a sevenfold vengeance." And the Lord put a mark on Cain, so that no one who came upon him would kill him. Then Cain went away from the presence of the Lord.

There are some very powerful spiritual symbolic lessons here, although this story is not meant as a literal account of an actual historic event. In fact, the story's full power and truth may not even have been in the minds of those who created it. Like many wonderful stories in the Bible, greater truths are revealed as human understanding increases.

Cain, the first-born who brought God an offering of vegetables, symbolizes an earlier stage of evolution. (Plant life preceded animal life.) Abel, the second-born, represents a later movement in evolution when animals appeared.

Abel's offering is found more pleasing—but don't believe for a minute that this is a true story about a God who is arbitrarily judging individuals and their offerings by preferences based on a humanlike personality. If that were the case, Cain had good reason to feel hurt and angry. He had brought the very best he could produce, and it seemed as though God had rejected it.

The real power of this story is in its symbolic representation of divine will, expressed through expansion and new forms of life as well as valuing that which has already been created. *The Lord said to Cain, "Why are you angry, and why has your countenance fallen? If you do well, will you not be accepted? And if you do not do well, sin [fear] is lurking at the door; its desire is for you, but you must master it."* Out of fear-based resentment, Cain kills his brother.

This story is highly symbolic of the hell that is created when passionate human beings resist evolving from fear to love and when the primate instinct for status is the ruling characteristic of relationships.

Cain was forgiven because he didn't understand; God allowed him to live so that humanity could continue on its course. While resistance to evolution produces suffering, progress in evolution reduces it, bringing hope, joy, and satisfaction into the human experience. This was evident in the nature of Jesus' ministry, teaching and work, and it should be evident in Christian religion. Very often, though, people who call themselves Christian resist its true message.

The satisfaction that comes from cooperating with our evolution toward Christhood creates peace and contentment within the human heart and within the conditions of the world while still allowing people to live passionate and exciting lives. Jesus dedicated his life to reducing suffering. He lived a highly passionate life.

In contrast, passionate efforts based on instincts result in suffering and what we call evil. Here are some examples:

o   The passionate effort to gain perfect physical security through accumulating wealth is expressed as **greediness**.
o   The passionate effort to prove one's superiority over others is expressed as **arrogance** and **pride**. When this instinct isn't satisfied, it can turn into **envy** and **jealousy**.
o   The passionate effort to gain satisfaction through consumption of food is **gluttony**. On an international level, it can result in the starvation of others.
o   The passionate effort to satisfy sexual or reproductive instinct results in all kinds of conditions that are harmful—**lust, rape, abuse, prostitution**, and countless **unhappy marriages**.
o   The passionate effort to raise or secure one's social position or establish a position of power or dominance over others results in **arrogance, oppression** and, very often, **violence**.

Jesus referred to these conditions when he spoke of the woes that would be experienced by corrupt Jewish religious leaders. In Matthew, Chapter 23: *"But woe to you, scribes and Pharisees, hypocrites! For you lock people out of the kingdom of heaven. For you do not go in yourselves, and when others are going in, you stop them. Woe to you, scribes and Pharisees, hypocrites! For you cross sea and land to make a single convert, and you make the new convert twice as much a child of hell as yourselves."*
Jesus is saying that life based on the satisfaction of maintaining prestige and power will always be unsatisfactory. He is also saying that religious leaders who do this with passion—crossing land and sea to make a convert—prevent themselves and others from experiencing

the next step in evolution, the Kingdom of Heaven. They make themselves and others residents of hell.

It's important to point out that Jesus was not faulting the religion of Judaism. He was referring to the passionate reactions of the human ego, which are expressed through all human conditions and religions.

In its divine expression passion is often called "compassion." The problem with this word is that it can be used to denote a superior/inferior relationship between people, as is sometimes seen in sympathy and charity toward the less fortunate. This doesn't mean that all people who help others are doing so just to prove their superiority. But recognition of status is often the object of some people who "do good."

Jesus understood that this condition was not helpful in the evolution into Christ consciousness. This is evidenced in his straight talk about alms-giving, which represented compassion in his day.

"So whenever you give alms, do not sound a trumpet before you, as the hypocrites do in the synagogues and in the streets, so that they may be praised by others. Truly I tell you, they have received their reward. But when you give alms, do not let your left hand know what your right hand is doing, so that your alms may be done in secret; and your Father who sees in secret will reward you." (Matthew 6:2)

True compassion recognizes the interdependence of all life—authentic good serves all while harm harms all—and the unity and spiritual equality of all people. Jesus referred to this equality in responding to disciples who argued among themselves about status.

A dispute also arose among them as to which one of them was to be regarded as the greatest. [The ego-based instinct for alpha status.] *But he said to them, "The kings of the Gentiles lord it over them; and those in authority over them are called benefactors. But not so with you; rather the greatest among you must become like the youngest, and the leader like one who serves. For who is greater, the one who is at the table or the one who serves? Is it not the one at the table? But I am among you as one who serves."* (Luke 22:24-27)

In the earlier stages of ego development, living passionately often meant living ambitiously, obsessively, or even fanatically in a world that could sometimes be hostile. It meant living in an environment of competing and conflicting self-interest with others.

Evolving into Christhood means living passionately and energetically in a world where each of us has a special role to bring God's love into greater expression in the human condition. Supporting and serving this purpose in one another makes this increasingly possible. It means to live in conscious awareness that God's will for mutual enhancement—love—is always the truth despite appearances to the contrary.

Jesus made the ultimate demonstration of that truth through his crucifixion and resurrection. It is the divine presence of passion that will bring your special gift to the world in extraordinary ways. Conflicting self-interests are replaced by relationships of interdependence, creating a harmony of activity, reduced stress, and greatly enhanced achievement. How to get there from here is the question. Step Nine is an essential part of the answer.

In previous steps, we looked at relationships in our lives and the root causes of pain and suffering we have experienced. Some of these relationships, we found, were resolved by one or both partners losing in a conflict that arose from a passionate pursuit of self-interest. Some relationships left us more skeptical about the presence of love in our world and more fearful about life. For many, the basis of these experiences existed in childhood events or relationships, locking us into patterns of conflict that continued to create suffering in later years.

We recognize that we cannot undo the past nor escape from it. But there is something we can do. In Step Nine we have the opportunity to add another chapter to these stories. The love of God is always present and always ready to create a relationship of mutual enhancement out of any experience, no matter how negative it was.

At this point many people ask why this needs to be done, particularly with people, situations, and conditions that no longer figure in our lives. Why not let sleeping dogs lie?

The best reason first: We are destined to have increased access to the power of the Christ for use in our personal lives the way Jesus used it in creating love and reducing human suffering.

As we have learned, this Christ consciousness is a state of great personal power created by the union of the personal mind with the divine mind. Since Christ power can only be used in the service of love, it is not available to individuals who believe in the reality of unresolved conflicts of self-interest with others. The transformation of these beliefs requires a very genuine and personal experience of granting and seeking forgiveness.

If the great power Jesus demonstrated was available to people who are still in an unresolved state of mind, they would use it to serve personal interests and easily become corrupted. Jesus was not corrupted because he had transcended the ego state of competing and conflicting self-interest.

Thus, there is no danger that Christ power can be misused. There is no fooling God into conferring Christ consciousness onto people before they are ready. It only emerges through divine order and can only be used for its true purpose, the creation of love.

When you get it, you can use it by simply affirming the reality of this power in bringing expression to the desires of the heart and mind. Jesus said so, as recorded in Mark, Chapter 11: *"Truly I tell you, if you say to this mountain, 'Be taken up and thrown into the sea,' and if you do not doubt in your heart, but believe that what you say will come to pass, it will be done for you."*

That is a great deal of power! I don't know if Jesus meant this literally or if he simply wanted to emphasize the extraordinary nature of this power.

Our commitment to seeking and attaining real forgiveness is a major factor determining how and when human consciousness will be transformed into Christ consciousness. Prayer is essential to these experiences. We need God's guidance in order to avoid further harm in situations that have been hurtful or highly charged.

In some cases no amend may be needed, such as when a person was a victim of random crime. A direct amend also is not appropriate where it would cause actual harm to others. However, in most cases where conflict occurred in an existing relationship, a direct amend that sweeps clean without finding fault will be very important to our transformation process. Here is an example from my life.

When working in management for a state health-care institution, I had a continuing conflict with my secretary. I felt she was trying to exercise excessive control over the way our office worked.

It was her job to provide support, but I believed she was deliberately sabotaging my effectiveness. Rather than follow my instructions, she actually took actions that were contrary to them. This made me very angry, and I retaliated—personally criticizing her and also gathering evidence and threatening to launch an effort to get her fired.

While considering making amends, I arrived at a different perspective. I became aware that I had felt insecure about my own job capabilities and feared my secretary had information that could get me fired. Her actions made me aware of how little control I had over her.

When I shared this revelation with my spiritual mentor, he reminded me that even if I were fired, this would not be a bad thing. It would have been God's way of moving me to a job that was more satisfying.

Acceptance of that truth released much of my fear. I realized how little I had been listening to my secretary. Instead, I had been trying to exercise excessive control myself—the very characteristic I projected on her.

When I made amends to her, I apologized for not valuing her input or listening to her. In the process I learned she had a difficult home life and tried to compensate by gaining satisfaction from her work. I saw how little I was concerned about how she could find the job more satisfying. My concern was based on my own self-centered fear and my desire for job satisfaction and control.

Free from fear, I was able to establish a new relationship with her based on mutual respect and cooperation. Her job satisfaction increased, the effectiveness of our department improved, and I liked coming to work a whole lot more.

Through our memory of outcomes, we create beliefs about the nature of life and relationships. If memories are colored exclusively by win or lose, we will believe that competition and fear-based self-interest are the only reality. If memories are colored by the presence of God's will for love in relationships, that becomes our reality.

Forgiveness, whether we seek it or confer it, changes our reality. It activates God's will for mutual enhancement and brings that will into expression. And it does so in a way that permanently changes our minds.

Our action allows that to happen. We are in charge of forgiveness. *But so that you may know that the Son of Man has authority on earth to forgive sins"—he said to the one who was paralyzed—"I say to you, stand up and take your bed and go to your home."* (Luke 5:24)

We are the Son of Man. Jesus transcended that reality to become a Son of God. It is up to us to bring forgiveness into the human experience.

The earlier quotation from the Gospel of Mark regarding the phenomenal power of prayer is immediately followed by *"...Whenever you stand praying, forgive, if you have anything against anyone; so that your Father in heaven may also forgive you your trespasses."*

Here again, Jesus addresses our role in change of consciousness and access to Christ power. He is saying that, as we assess our lives and bring forgiveness into our experiences, we will know a new way to be in harmony with ourselves, with creation, and with God's will for love. We will have made ourselves available for the activity of the divine mind to work in our personal lives, creating connections of mutual enhancement from every experience.

The more we ask God to help bring forgiveness into our lives and the more we cooperate by seeking and granting forgiveness, the more our minds will be changed. Then we will become free from limitations created by the law of cause and effect and from the temptation of winning and losing. We will move closer to our transformation into Christ consciousness—access to a new and incorruptible power through personal union with the mind of God.

In altering the outcome of past stories that make up our experience, we begin to see and feel big changes. New degrees of peace often flood into our minds and hearts. Everything we need to live these new lives seems to come with much greater ease. A greater faith than ever before is ours.

This is a process, and we just need to hang in there as it continues to unfold. We will be entering into a time of change—no longer our old selves and yet not evolved into the full expression of our Christ nature. We need strength during this time. Strength is the next faculty of mind.

In Step Ten, we will find a new kind of strength that makes it possible for us to grow and change with a marked reduction in pain and suffering and a greatly increased capacity to create good.

Chapter Ten

STRENGTH

*In the **Tenth Step**, we continue to take personal inventory and promptly admit when we are wrong.*

S tep Nine marked completion of the second phase of the transformation process, in which we experienced very real change in our minds and hearts. This change was felt as a new peace of mind. We gained access to a new creative power. We began being reborn into a new state of consciousness.

Strength is the enduring faculty of mind in which continuous and sustained energy is expressed, carrying life forward in its evolutionary path to Christ consciousness. **Andrew is the apostle.**

In Steps Ten, Eleven, and Twelve we will be harvesting the fruits of our work to date. The Kingdom of Heaven will become increasingly visible in our world and in the stories of our lives. In these steps we will address the ways each of us fulfill our purposes in life through the continued evolutionary journey into Christ consciousness.

In this final phase of the transformation process let's remind ourselves of the premises stated in the Introduction to the Twelve Steps. These premises are based on the following truths.

Every person has taken on elements of human nature, as it currently exists, for the ultimate purpose of moving humanity and ourselves forward in the evolutionary journey toward conscious unity with God.

After completing the life review phase, our emerging Christ nature begins to play a larger and more satisfying role in interactions with people in our lives. Current relationships begin to change, if they

93

haven't done so already. The strength faculty of mind addressed in Step Ten lends support as we apply the Christ principles to our lives.

Through spiritual evolution, each life becomes an expression of the emerging divine sense of self, demonstrating the glory of God and God's will for the creation of new expressions of love and abundant life.

We have inherited special gifts that will bless us and others and will demonstrate the glory and love of God expressed through our emerging Christ nature. The expression of this gift provides great personal satisfaction. It always benefits others. The mind faculty of vision or imagination, which is God's vision of you, will be required to fulfill this purpose. Step Eleven will address that process.

By Step Twelve we will have awakened to our emerging Christ nature and tapped into the power of God that enables the creative expression of that nature as the unfolding stories of our life.

A crucial element of that awakening is the discovery of the unique ways we are to assist others in the transformation process. With minds and hearts transformed, we find that God's promise of peace, harmony, fulfillment, and abundant life are true for us today. Step Twelve completes the circle and brings us back to life, to a life transformed. The Kingdom of God is at hand. Our newfound conscious unity with God is expressed as creative power in our lives.

Throughout this transformation, we are required to expand our understanding of self. We now need to know ourselves as individual spiritual components of the one divine life energy.

At this point in the process, we no longer see ourselves as victims but as people who have inherited some aspect of human nature—not for punishment but for the purpose of transforming it through authentic, personal, spiritual growth. We have gained unique personality traits and characteristics, within which lie the seeds of our own special gifts. We will deal with the growth and harvest of these gifts in Steps Eleven and Twelve.

The characteristics of the individual natures we will be transforming have been handed down generation to generation for as long as humans have walked the Earth. Actually, many of them have their roots in the planet's earliest evolving life forms. How they have come to us—whether through genetics, culture, or reincarnation—isn't clear yet. But it is evident they predate the emergence of our species.

Let's briefly consider the idea of reincarnation and the nature of eternal life.

Are we—our souls—the reincarnation of previous existences? I like the way one of my spiritual instructors described his thinking. He said he didn't believe in reincarnation in his last life and he doesn't believe in it in this one either! Many people consider reincarnation an unknowable mystery. Others seem very sure, meaning they are positive it is true or they are positive it isn't true.

I tend to believe in reincarnation, though not in the linear way many people in the Western world do. I believe that my life energy is part of a universal energy that expresses itself in a multitude of organic life forms we define as species and individuals.

I also believe that all life energy, whether in organic form or not, is eternal. None is lost; it simply reverts back to an unformed state upon physical death and takes form again through new birth.

You can use the analogy of water and ice cubes to understand this a bit better. When you make ice cubes, water molecules take on an individual identity as an ice cube. Melting, the ice cube returns to a state of unity with all water. The individual ice cube is not a specific reincarnation of earlier cubes, but the molecules that make up the water have existed in many previous forms.

Similarly, our life energy—biologically expressed in the DNA it creates—is reincarnated into new individual forms with slight variations in different incarnations. Contained within these ongoing life energy patterns is information accumulated from the history of past individuals through which our species is evolving.

It is worth noting that life energy isn't lost even when a species becomes extinct. It reverts to a condition where it becomes available for new or different species identification.

In human beings, a new dimension has been added—the potential for an ongoing individual identity even after death. That potential is fulfilled through the transformation of life energy, the soul, into Christ consciousness. As the true offspring of God, Christ has an eternal life as an individual creative component of the divine mind.

The seed of that eternal individual identification exists in each of us. It is the light of life that has existed since the very beginning of life on our planet. There is a reference to this in John, Chapter 1. *He was in the beginning with God... What has come into being in him was life, and the life was the light of all people.*

In this passage, individual Christ consciousness is identified as the potential and purpose of evolution. According to Jesus, this has always been the purpose of God, and Jesus introduced it into the reality of the human condition.

That's the good news of the Gospel. Each time human life energy is born into physical form, it carries the potential for evolution into Christhood. *"For God so loved the world that he gave his only Son, so that everyone who believes in him may not perish but may have eternal life."* (John 3:16)

The Christ potential in the human being is the Child of God. Through its realization, the Kingdom of God is brought into the world. *"...He gave power to become children of God, who were born, not of blood or of the will of the flesh or of the will of man, but of God. And the Word became flesh and lived among us, and we have seen his glory, the glory as of a father's only son, full of grace and truth."* (John 1:12)

Jesus, a human being in full Christ consciousness, retained his identity as an individual concentration of life energy following his experience on the cross. This was shown by his almost immediate resurrection and appearance. Since that time, countless people have sworn to having experienced his living presence.

The life energy of every person continues on after death. It is either assimilated back into the human pattern for new expression and evolution or it retains an eternal identity based on evolution into Christ consciousness.

The fear of losing our identity is what humans find so painful. We are designed for eternal life as individuals. We are being drawn to it by the presence of the Christ within us. Anything less is unsatisfactory.

In this model of eternal life, reincarnation is likely to be experienced as either the memories of physical life that exist within the overall pattern of human life or as the ongoing individual identity of the Christ. This would be consistent with Jesus' teachings. In Step Ten we continue the evolution of our consciousness, but our focus is now on the present rather than the past.

As stated earlier, each of us has a God-ordained, spiritual mission to take on the human condition for the purpose of evolution toward Christhood. Individuals who are ready and willing to follow the teachings of Jesus have everything they need to carry out this mission, including the strength given by God.

Everyone "takes on" some form of ego-based fear. Whether disease, physical limitation, poverty, oppression; dependency, victimization, domination, aggression; isolation, addiction, shame, guilt, or hatred. In taking on the human condition, we do not simply learn about some aspect of humanity. This is a real experience, not an intellectual exercise. Through it we have become what we are—and this is what we will evolve.

There will be a great temptation to try to see how others need to evolve—thus avoiding facing ourselves and our own purpose. But we must deal with our own humanity first. And, undeniably, that can be a job.

In Steps Eight and Nine we dealt with conflicts in our past through forgiveness. In Step Ten, we continue the process on a day-to-day basis, calling on the mind faculty of strength to persevere.

Because of the life review, we are now better able to recognize conflicting or competing self-interest. We have become very sensitive to suffering caused by fear-based states of mind. At the same time, we may notice that all of the suffering hasn't gone away. Some of our old ideas seem to resurface once in a while, and they make us quite uncomfortable. We notice that the road has indeed narrowed.

"Enter through the narrow gate; for the gate is wide and the road is easy that leads to destruction, and there are many who take it. For the gate is narrow and the road is hard that leads to life." (Matthew 7:13,14)

We know we are not expected to be perfect. We are in a state of evolution. We can actually be grateful for discomfort because each experience brings opportunities to experience new degrees of transformation, peace, and abundant life.

In Step Ten we recognize the strength of God, which allows us to continue in the spiritual growth process with vastly reduced suffering. As we become less interested in finding victory in relationships, it becomes easier to acknowledge our individual ego-based or primate characteristics when they are exposed.

It is important to recognize here the qualities of strength needed for this stage of growth and to understand the difference between ego-based strength and spiritual strength.

Strength has always been related to the capacity to endure and overcome. In John, Chapter 16, Jesus says, *"...In me you may have peace. In the world you face persecution. But take courage; I have conquered the world!"* His peaceful overcoming of the world was the result of divine strength, which is the nature of love.

In the past, strength nearly always denoted some kind of victory over a condition in which defeat was possible. It is easily identified—even worshipped—in many competitive sports and continues to be highly valued in most cultures.

In most affairs of human beings, mental strength has replaced physical strength. To quote the 19th-century English novelist Edward Bulwer-Lytton: *"The pen is mightier than the sword."* Mental strength has also been useful in amplifying physical strength. The bulldozer, created through the use of expanded mental energy, can move much more earth than a person with a stick. A nuclear bomb can kill many more people than a thrown rock.

The story of David and Goliath is a striking Old Testament example of mind over matter. David, the physical underdog, triumphed by recognizing his foe's vulnerability and devising an imaginative solution. His unique approach is recognized as a gift of God. It represented a step in evolution, and all steps in evolution are gifts of God.

Of course, David used his newfound strength to gain victory in a conflict of self-interest between himself and Goliath—between the Israelites and the Philistines. This was not the same strength Jesus understood and used. The ideas of victory and defeat, so much a part of early human evolution, must eventually be surrendered in order to access the greater strength of the Christ.

This change is evident in the way Jesus advocated forgiving one's enemies rather than defeating them. That makes perfect sense when you understand the move in the evolution from relationships of conflicting self-interest to relationships of mutual enhancement. This move cannot be made while you still see life from the perspective of a separate self, experiencing life as victory or defeat.

When we rely on God's strength, rather than physical or mental strength, we avail ourselves of a new and wondrous power and with it we can experience a state of unusual peace in the middle of what might be great conflict. This is the kind of strength we gain access to in Step Ten.

As the situations and conditions of our lives unfold on a daily basis, we will be exposed to potential conflict. Indeed, this will be true for as long as we are active in the world, and there will be a temptation to use ego-based strength to deal with it. This will be especially true when victory seems highly possible or when we or our loved ones are threatened by some form of injustice.

When we turn to the presence of the Christ within us, rely on the activity of God in the world, and refuse to participate based on victory or defeat, we experience the strength of God. We will be cooperating and experiencing a transformation of the human condition. In making these responses, we begin to appreciate the wondrous ways that God works in the world.

We will find many opportunities to do that in our daily lives—for example, when driving on a busy freeway. In the past, that's where I most frequently became aware of my primate nature! It's easy to get caught up in feelings of competition or conflicts of interest with other motorists. You jockey for position. You get cut off. Incased in steel and glass, at the controls of a great deal of power, you feel isolated and separate. It's easy to see why tempers flair.

If that happens, there is no need to be disappointed with yourself or judgmental of others. We simply need to recognize that this characteristic is part of human nature and ask God to help transform this state of mind. If certain patterns of conflict repeat themselves, it usually means we need to bring forgiveness into some earlier event that was responsible for the fear that supports these patterns. It may require revisiting the earlier life review steps.

Calling on God and recognizing the power of the emerging Christ, we easily access the strength to persevere with the transformation process. Part of this divine strength may come through others' help. Counseling, when it focuses on discovering areas of life that need to have forgiveness applied, is very effective and usually speeds the process.

Forgiveness must always be the goal, and unfortunately that isn't the goal of every counselor. To find the right person, ask for God's guidance and then use honest discussion to determine whether the counselor understands and is sympathetic with this spiritual approach.

As a result of the steps to date, we have a new understanding of humanity. We know we have the purpose and resources to deal with transformation with a minimum of pain and suffering.

We will now put it to the test. This is analogous to Jesus' experience in the wilderness just before he began demonstrating Christ powers in his ministry. Step Ten represents our wilderness experience.

Temptation will certainly be part of it. We will be tempted to revert to old, primate-based ways, but we will have the strength to continue. In so doing, we will realize we are receiving everything we need. As they did for Jesus, the angels will wait on us.

And a voice came from heaven, "You are my Son, the Beloved; with you I am well pleased." And the Spirit immediately drove him out into the wilderness. He was in the wilderness forty days, tempted by Satan; and he was with the wild beasts; and the angels waited on him. (Mark 1:11-13)

In this new state of mind, we are no longer hard on others or ourselves. Neither are we in denial about human nature as we continue to evaluate the way we experience life. We know that transformation into Christ consciousness is an evolutionary process and that we have a loving God as our director. We can fearlessly face the appearance of evil, for we have found a state of peace and serenity and a new spiritual strength that will serve us on a daily basis.

We are on the way. We are becoming ready to bring our gift—our true Christ nature—into greater expression in the world. In expressing our unique individuality, we go beyond the healing focus of transformation into the experience of co-creating with God the abundance of all that is good in life. *Finally!*

Jesus said that God's purpose in initiating this next step in evolution was to bring abundant life. In this next step, the glory of God will be brought abundantly into the world, through the Christ in each of us. True satisfaction and joy in life are now available.

Imagine that! Are you ready?

Chapter Eleven

IMAGINATION

*In the **Eleventh Step,** we seek through prayer and meditation to increase our conscious contact with God as we understand God, praying only for the knowledge of God's will for us and the power to carry that out.*

Throughout these steps we have held onto (sometimes just barely) a fundamental idea: God's will for love is present everywhere at all times, regardless of how things temporarily appear.

Imagination is the faculty of mind in which mental energy is shaped into images or descriptions of conditions for future physical manifestation. **Bartholomew is the apostle.**

If you are anything like me, maintaining this state of mind can sometimes be a challenge. It is very possible you have experienced lapses back to the state from which we are evolving, where fears associated with the ego sense of self seem to be the truth of life.

Even if you have affirmed the presence of God, you may have applied more mental and emotional energy to the appearance of conflict and threat than to the truth of God's presence. An ongoing personal evaluation through the use of Step Ten will give you an idea of where you are.

Again, if you're anything like me—and you truly want to make progress toward Christ consciousness—you may be somewhat disappointed in yourself. But let me tell you: This is the biggest waste of time. Don't dwell on it.

We are all at a specific point in our evolution. Most of us have a ways to go, and getting down on ourselves will only slow progress. But also be honest about where you are and your ongoing need for growth. This is crucial.

In our old state, we are highly aware of the genetic/biological and cultural influences that make up our subconscious mind. Think about the human condition. The potential to express the Christ was planted in human beings at some point after we emerged from the primate state. Imagination and its resulting creative responses to life are early characteristics of this emerging Christ nature.

The growth in human creative activity has accelerated tremendously in the past 35,000 years. Moreover, we are the product of five billion years of successful struggle to survive, evolve, and reproduce—the story of life on Earth. All that got us here and is to be honored. But we need to move on.

The state of consciousness we are now entering is the realization of the divine spark of Christ as the essence of our being and the realization that struggle is no longer the most effective way to create our lives. In this state we become aware that the presence of God and the potential for greater expressions of God's love are the real nature and purpose of all existence. In our personal lives it means a new way of being free from struggle.

"Take my yoke upon you, and learn from me; for I am gentle and humble in heart, and you will find rest for your souls. For my yoke is easy, and my burden is light." (Matthew 11:29,30)

Most of us will move back and forth between these two states, at least for the time being. I see old ideas of mine that still seem to dominate at times. At the same time, I see within myself a growing awareness of the Christ.

Occasionally, I fear that my old self might win and I want to defeat it. I want to defeat any negative thinking or feeling that seems to draw me into competition and conflicts of self-interest with others. I would like to use my Christ power to annihilate things that seem wrong with me!

This desire is understandable. It is based on the current state of evolution and on the earlier state of primate consciousness. But as Jesus' parable of the wheat field (quoted in Chapter Four) indicates, the seeds of Christ consciousness have been planted and are growing.

The seeds of conflict arising from our attempts at instinct satisfaction sometimes seem to be growing, too, and they may look like a real threat to the promises of Christ. It sometimes seems the weeds are choking out the wheat. The temptation is to get in there and clear them out!

But hold on. All will be resolved in good time. Those aspects of consciousness that no longer nourish us will be disposed of. We need not worry too much about them now. (A pretty radical idea in this age of self-improvement, isn't it?)

We must focus on the "wheat"—the indwelling Christ nature—and see it growing and maturing, so we will be in a position to gather the fruits of Christ consciousness that are maturing in the fields of our minds.

Strength does not come through our capacity to defeat the bad seed. It comes from the presence of love that nourishes the good seed as it grows in our mind. That strength—love—is accessed best through prayer and meditation. That is the new kind of strength we tapped during Step Ten and now rely on totally in Step Eleven. It is the strength of the Christ who is fully at one with God. It is the actual strength of the presence of God at the very center of our being. It is the essence of our existence.

With this in mind we can begin evaluating how we spend our mental energy. Prayer and meditation are expenditures of mental energy. So are fear, worry, and resentment.

Though we are not completely free of worry and resentment, we can turn from them whenever we choose and focus our minds on the indwelling Christ. Though we are not yet ready to totally eliminate the seeds of conflict, we can bring degrees of change through affirming God's presence, applying our new understanding of ourselves and others, and seeking/conferring forgiveness.

We don't need to punish or destroy the weeds. In fact, to the degree that we try to do that, we only impede our own progress. What we can do is affirm and practice the state of mind in which we surrender to the Christ. Through this, we can know that the infinite wisdom and will of God will respond to every unfolding condition in our world. The weeds of negativity will eventually die and then can be bundled up and disposed of.

Harvest time is determined by the degree of Christ consciousness emerging in each individual. In the Gospels, it was emerging much faster in Jesus' disciples than in other people of that time. The teachings that were directed toward the disciples were different from the teachings and parables directed toward the masses. This is because Jesus was preparing the disciples for a more immediate entrance into this next stage of evolution. *"But truly I tell you, there are some standing here who will not taste death before they see the kingdom of God."* (Luke 9:27)

He also gave teachings to the public, even though the majority of people didn't understand them. He did so knowing that the teachings would remain, that humanity as a whole would eventually follow the course his disciples were taking. We are now becoming privy to the true meaning and implication of that.

As this new understanding of Jesus' life and teachings dawns on us, we should realize we are in a state of evolution similar to what the disciples were experiencing. He told them that the harvest was at hand: *"...Do you not say, 'Four months more, then comes the harvest'? But I tell you, look around you, and see how the fields are ripe for harvesting."* (John, Chapter 4).

Jesus uses the visionary words "look" and "see." He asks us to see something that is not necessarily apparent physically. He communicates by metaphor, pointing to recently planted fields and sprouting wheat. (He says it is four months to harvest). He does this to signal the possibility that humans can enter the Kingdom of Heaven much sooner than anyone would have imagined.

Who at that time, or even now, knew the potential inherent in the Christ nature that is hidden within the souls of human beings? Who knew it even existed? The answer is: very few, beyond a few prophets and holy men of various religions.

It has been part of human nature, only hidden, since humanity emerged from the primate level of evolution. As stated in John 1:9,10: *The true light, which enlightens everyone, was coming into the world. He was in the world, and the world came into being through him; yet the world did not know him.* Likewise in Luke 8:17: *For nothing is hidden that will not be disclosed, nor is anything secret that will not become known and come to light.*

The Christ potential has been growing in the human condition for thousands, if not millions, of years and now is coming into its own. Jesus was one of the first great harvesters. His disciples were next. Very possibly, it is your turn now.

In Matthew, Chapter 9, Jesus said: *"The harvest is plentiful, but the laborers are few."* Christianity in its true form—its spiritual form—is about recruiting laborers, those who will harvest God's will for abundant life and love in this world through personal transformation.

We are now reaping what others have sown. This may sound as though the untold numbers of human beings who lived and died without this experience are left out. But in Christ—in God—there is no separation through time or space; there is only one life energy taking many forms.

All life energy is ultimately unified in God. All human life energy will eventually be transformed into full Christ consciousness through its continuing re-creation in individual forms. As these souls evolve into Christ consciousness, their identities as individuals become eternal. At the same time, they remain in full and loving unity with all other life, with creation, and with God.

Thus, the sower and the reaper are joined. *The reaper is already receiving wages and is gathering fruit for eternal life, so that sower and reaper may rejoice together.* (John 4:36) The way Jesus puts it, it seems to be a promise meant to come true in this lifetime. As always, you and I have a role to play. And the way we play our roles determines, at least to some degree, the time of harvest for us.

The greatest temptation we will have is to go on a weed-pulling spree—to remove characteristics easily identified with previous stages of evolution. Our role will be to resist that temptation.

That may seem contrary to most traditional Christian teachings, even contrary to common sense. But I don't believe it is contrary to what Jesus taught. Let us not go to war with ourselves, our old natures, or other people. The attempt to defeat evil reflects a belief that evil is a real power—but that belief is the only power it has.

That is the basis for Jesus' emphasis on loving your enemy, on forgiveness, and on not contending with the appearance of evil. What is essential is that the Christ continues to emerge. In doing so, it will overcome all else through forgiveness and love.

Remember in Steps Six and Seven, when we decided to let God determine how our particular quirks of character would be dealt with? Well, we need to continually renew that decision. Our mental and spiritual energy needs to be redirected away from self-improvement and directed toward God consciousness (which is, of course, Christ consciousness).

Step Eleven says: "Seek through prayer and meditation to improve our conscious contact with God, as we understand God, praying only for the knowledge of God's will for us and the power to carry that out." Notice there is nothing here about pulling weeds or self-improvement. It is about gaining a greater understanding of God's will for us so that the time of harvest will be made known.

Of course, greater conscious contact with God will also reduce the pain and suffering caused by the continued, temporary presence of weeds in our consciousness. The good news is that it will do much more than that.

o It will disclose the exact and unique nature of the Christ essence that exists as the core of your individuality.
o It will reveal your unique gift to life and to the human condition.
o It will provide you with a new vision of yourself, a vision that will be a blessing to you and to the world.

From this new vision will emerge a powerful capacity to create unique connections of mutual enhancement in relationships with other people. This is a new and wonderful way of imagining life. It is the very essence of Step Eleven.

One of my first experiences with this kind of vision happened when I was introduced to these teachings through the Unity movement. I was in Southern California and had been on a spiritual journey for a number of years. In the preface to this book, I talked briefly about the confusion of my early life. I had grown up in the Catholic Church but rejected it as a teenager. Later I tried the

Methodist Church, the Lutheran Church, and other churches that were more evangelical and fundamentalist.

I had been prayed over, confirmed, promised the reward of heaven, and threatened with eternity in hell. But little of it had any real, positive effect on my spiritual journey. Still, I intuitively sensed that I was born into Christianity for some reason and that "something" existed "somewhere" that would help me in my journey, even though it was hidden from me so far.

While in California, I met a number of people who suggested I try the Unity Church. They said I talked the way they did at Unity. Eventually I decided to try it, assuming that if it was similar to my spirituality, it couldn't be Christian oriented. Imagine my surprise and disappointment when I drove by the church and read its sign—Christ Unity Church. I didn't bother to go in.

Finally, a friend talked me into attending a service with her. My mind hadn't changed, but I figured I could put up with anything for an hour. (And, anyway, she happened to be quite attractive!)

Five minutes into that service, I realized this was what I had craved. I intuitively knew that my Christian heritage was about to be reconciled with my emerging spiritual beliefs. I had discovered a spiritual, rather than a religious, approach to Christianity.

In another few minutes I had an overwhelming vision in which I would dedicate my life's work to this movement. (As a child I had a similar vision of myself as a Catholic priest.) However, it didn't take long for me to discount that vision. I thought I was simply not the ministerial type. Besides, I had my mind set on a career in graphic design.

I stayed in the Unity Church as a layperson, and as I continued to study and pray, it wasn't long before I had an even stronger vision. In this one, I was to follow Jesus into the wilderness for the purpose of accessing a new divine power, like he did. "Now there's a fantasy!" my rational mind warned. "It's one you better keep to yourself or they will lock you up with the rest of the mentally ill!" Nevertheless, the visions wouldn't go away.

God knows I resisted those visions—for years. I went on to become successful in the graphic arts field as a competent, though not gifted, designer. I had a somewhat successful custom sign and display business.

All the time I was pursuing my graphic arts career, I continued to study the spiritual path, particularly the approach to Christianity I found in Unity. After a couple of years, I felt guided to move to Ames, Iowa. I thought this guidance was strictly about business—that Ames seemed a good place for a sign and display business. And it was. The business financially supported me. What it didn't give me was any true sense of satisfaction.

Ames had no Unity Church, which was another thing that baffled me about the seeming guidance I had received. After living there for a couple of years, I decided to start a study group. As soon as I made a personal commitment to that idea, the vision of working full time in the movement flooded in again, much stronger than before. This time I paid attention to it.

I found the perfect buyer for my business, meaning I could work part-time for him while starting the Unity study group and pursuing my formal education in Unity teachings. Events continued to unfold in wondrous ways, supporting my new endeavors and the growth of the study group. All of the right people seemed to show up. Soon I began working full time as the spiritual leader of the Unity Church of Ames.

Still, the vision about following Jesus into the wilderness didn't go away. Frankly, it seemed as outrageous as ever, but something else was happening. My ministry was not feeling exactly right to me. Finally I figured it out. I had a question about the "God-human-Jesus" relationship, and to continue in the role of spiritual leadership, I needed to find the answer. The question was this:

*"If Jesus meant that, in following him, we were to become like him—divine in nature, at one with God, with the power to reduce human suffering and create expressions of love and abundant life at will, using the divinely enhanced powers of mind he exhibited...***then why isn't anyone doing it?"**

In John 14:12, Jesus says: *"Very truly, I tell you, the one who believes in me will also do the works that I do and, in fact, will do greater works than these."* With all my heart I wanted to believe in this Christ nature emerging in human beings. I had dedicated my life to teaching it as the ultimate truth for human beings.

So why hadn't it happened to me? Why hadn't it happened to anyone I knew, including all of the wonderful ministers of various denominations I had encountered? I personally knew of nobody who could perform the miracles or elicit the response of faith that Jesus did. I knew of nobody who consistently performed the healing that Jesus seemed to do. I knew of absolutely nobody who was doing miracles like the loaves and fishes, the walking on water, the changing of water to wine, the bringing a dead person back to life.

Why was this so? If what we were teaching was true and if Jesus said the Kingdom of Heaven was at hand, why wasn't anyone doing it?

True, there are many positive things that happen to people who practice affirmative prayer and meditation. I know of a number of synchronous occurrences in my life and in the lives of other people that have the appearance and feel of the miraculous. But they seem to be sporadic and not often available when people seem to need them most.

I've seen people who weren't addicted to negative thinking easily give up negative reactions to conditions and experience definite improvements in the quality of their lives. I've also seen people spend years with these teachings and never free themselves of negative, fear-based thought patterns or destructive habits. I saw myself in the latter category, even while trying to teach the Unity way of life.

Was there something inherently wrong with humans that kept them from entering into the full expression of Christ? If true, that would mean Unity was very possibly wrong in its basic theology because it teaches that human beings are inherently good. *God saw everything that he had made, and indeed, it was very good.* (Genesis 1:31)

If there was something inherently wrong with humans—or if there was some historical event created by human beings or by God that brought on human suffering—then I probably couldn't continue in this work.

I pondered other theories. Could it mean there was another power in the universe (the "devil" of Christianity)? Could it be that God wasn't truly omnipresent in the physical world or perhaps wasn't all good? All of these ideas ran contrary to my own experiences of revelation and to those things I was trying to believe and teach. I knew I needed some sort of satisfactory answer, so I decided to take a three-month sabbatical.

I had been working very hard for three years as spiritual leader of Unity of Ames and as business manager of the Unity Church of Des Moines. I was tired. As usual, things came together to make it possible to take time off. That helped make it obvious to me that something was working in the spiritual realm, though nothing to the degree that Jesus experienced.

In retrospect, it looks like I headed off into the wilderness. I decided that I would do nothing but ask my question of God and wait for the answer. Through prayer, meditation, and maybe even confrontation, I would seek to improve my conscious contact with God, praying only for the real knowledge of God's will and how that could be carried out.

Certainly there is a place for strength and persistence in the spiritual path. It is not in attempting to force something, but always in prayer and meditation and in never giving up on asking God. The answer came, and I have written in this book as it was revealed to me.

We are not denied Christ power because we are bad. We are denied it simply because we are not yet ready for it—similarly to a young teenager being denied control of a powerful motor vehicle. We have not fully grown into the level of spiritual maturity where we could use that extraordinary creative power the way God intended.

God is a living presence. The divine desire to create ever-greater expressions of love and abundant life has always been active in the world. Death has never been a reality. No life energy is ever lost, and no human life energy will ever be permanently excluded from the Kingdom of Heaven.

The ideas and beliefs that supported earlier stages of human evolution, but are no longer useful, will eventually go up in spiritual smoke. All human life energy will one day become conscious of its divine, eternal nature. When this happens—or as it happens—a few million or billion new expressions of God will take their place as unique creative components of the divine mind, co-creating the ongoing evolution of the universe.

Ultimately, that transformation is the personal vision I have for myself. It is the one that God placed in me. The one I had about following Jesus into the wilderness and becoming like him is my true vision. So is the one I am expressing in service to the Unity movement today. Serving in a spiritual leadership role is simply part of my unique way of moving forward in the fulfillment of that vision. The work I am doing serves that vision at this time—weeds (and there are plenty of them) and all!

All human beings, Christian or not, will ultimately become aware of their divine natures. Each will have the power to express God in the world in a unique and mutually enhancing way.

How close is it? I don't know, but my sense is that it is close. That's what Jesus said and I believe him.

How does it feel to you? When you consider this question, try to reduce your anxiety about weeds in your own consciousness. Though it is essential to accept their existence, they are not all that important.

What about your vision? Do you have a sense that something beyond your wildest dreams could happen or is happening to you? Is there a vision that would satisfy the craving of your heart? My belief for you is that there is.

Can you be persistent in your prayer and meditation and insist on getting an answer? I believe you are here in this place, at this time, being exposed to the teachings of Jesus in this way, because your time is close at hand. You have a new kind of strength, and you have a divinely inspired vision deep within yourself waiting to emerge.

Through you—*the Christ in you*—your life is designed to be transformed. Through us—*the Christ in us*—the world and humanity can and will be transformed and we will live on in eternal creative harmony in a universe of love. The power is here and available now.

For many people the question will be "How do I pray and meditate in ways that truly bring me the knowledge of God's will and the power to carry that out?" Let's first explore meditation.

Meditation is a form of daily surrender, and it's needed because we live in two dimensions. One dimension, which we addressed in the life review steps, unfolds from the past into the future. The other dimension, which becomes important in Step Eleven, is "in the moment," providing access to infinite depths of spirit, the living presence of God, our Christ nature.

The specific way individuals meditate varies a great deal. There are many, many books on techniques, and it's important that you find ones that work for you. It's also important that you be willing to change techniques as you mature spiritually. As with all ways of being, you are likely to grow out of ones that served you in the past. If you ask, God will continually guide you in finding ways to meditate.

You can tell if a technique is right for you by the degree of release from concerns and fears you experience. Meditation does not increase the Christ presence; it simply releases us from worry and fear so that the Christ within us can emerge as new ideas, vision, and purpose.

It is through meditation that we become aware of our intuition and begin to rely on its amazing ability to guide us, and there are numerous ways to practice it. Sitting in silence, chanting, walking, ecstatic dancing, rocking, visualizing, focusing, making art, listening to music, writing—and these are just a few. Some are aural, some are visual, some are kinesthetic.

Most have been highly effective for certain people, though none of them works for everyone. That's why I stress the importance of experimenting until you find the ones that allow you to withdraw mental and emotional energy from the past and the future and become fully present and at peace in the moment. That is how we access God through our indwelling Christ nature. The more we become peaceful and free of anxiety and struggle the greater access we have. That's the goal of meditation and it works!

As we practice Step Eleven and continue to find our own unique way to meditate, to access the deepest place of truth within us, we will tap a new level of life energy. It is the purest of all energies, the life, love, and wisdom of God, and it will begin to radiate from the center of our being to permeate our minds and hearts.

Prayer serves two purposes. It allows us to consciously bring the pure energy of God into focus in the unfolding stories of our lives, and it allows us to deny creative power to any fear reactions we may still harbor. With faith and with freedom from fear and struggle we ask for and accept the intuitive guidance that directs our actions and responses.

We know that our lives are meant to express God's will for expanding good, and we sense that we now have access to a kind of wonderful new power to make it happen. This power never requires us to enter into win/lose competition or conflict with others.

Affirmative prayer is the application of the living energy of God expressed in the story of our lives. Because life will still present conditions and situations that appear to be "against us," we use denial prayer to remove the creative energy of our mind from reacting to these conditions.

We don't deny that problems exist. We just deny that seemingly negative and destructive appearances are the ultimate reality, and we refuse to use our mental and emotional energy as if they are! We know the truth of God's love and we affirm that—no matter what life appears to be like in the moment. This works!

In Step Ten we began to use that energy to change the way we respond to the situations in our life. Our minds and our lives are right now being transformed. Now, in Step Eleven, we begin to look to the living presence of God within us for a new and powerful way to envision our future.

Through this transformation we will become aware of our unique purpose and mission in life. These will bring joy, satisfaction, great peace, and the truest experience of love possible—the answer to all of our desires.

With the Christ vision and the activity of God's love transforming our lives, we will gain access to a new creative power. The power to bring our Christ nature into physical expression in the world is the next and final step in this cycle of evolution into the Kingdom of Heaven. In Step Twelve, we will come full circle back to life.

If you have followed these steps—doing the work of surrender, inventory, sharing, forgiveness, prayer, and meditation—you have experienced some degree of spiritual transformation. Now you are coming back into the circle of life a different person.

You and I are becoming empowered with a new degree of the Christ. As St. Paul said, the Christ within us is our hope for glory. *To them God chose to make known how great among the Gentiles are the riches of the glory of this mystery, which is Christ in you, the hope of glory.* (Colossians 1:27)

Chapter Twelve

POWER

*In the **Twelfth Step**, having had a spiritual awakening as the result of these steps, we try to carry this message to others and to practice these principles in all of our affairs.*

F*or Thine is the Kingdom, the Power and the Glory, for ever and ever, Amen.* So goes the last line of the beloved Lord's Prayer. As we come into a new state of conscious union with the divine mind, there is no longer a question about who we are and what the nature of our relationship is with God. There is no longer God **and** us. There is only God.

We are increasingly aware that we are unique and creative expressions of the ultimate living truth. And from that awakened awareness, it is simple to understand, affirm, and love the last statement of the Lord's Prayer. When we begin to know ourselves as the Christ, God's kingdom, power, and glory are not separate from us. They become the truth of our lives.

The fact is, there has never been a true separation between God and us. God has always been the only power and presence in the universe. Most of us, with conscious minds informed by the ego sense of self, were simply not aware of that, or at least not aware of the full implications of what it could mean in our lives.

Even so, life as a whole and each of us individually have been playing a role in humanity's evolution toward Christ consciousness. As our role becomes clear,

Power is the faculty of mind in which formed mental energy is effortlessly brought into physical manifestation as actions, conditions, relationships and supply of all that is needed to further the mission of the individual and the evolution of humanity into Christhood. **Philip is the apostle.**

our unity with God and all life is realized at depth.

The three key words in the last line of the Lord's Prayer appear frequently in the four gospels. In the New Revised Standard Version, the word "kingdom" appears 123 times, the words "power" or "authority," 75 times; the word "glory," 71 times.

Jesus used the words "kingdom of heaven" (in the book of Matthew) and "kingdom of God" (in all four gospels) to describe this future state of consciousness that is the destiny of humankind. In this state, new levels of Christ Power or Divine Authority become our personal reality.

It is a very recognizable power, as those who encountered Jesus attested. *On the Sabbath he began to teach in the synagogue, and many who heard him were astounded. They said, "Where did this man get all this? What is this wisdom that has been given to him? What deeds of power are being done by his hands!"* (Mark 6:2)

Those who knew Jesus only as the local carpenter's son were especially amazed. In Matthew 13:55, this reaction is recorded: *Is not this the carpenter's son? Is not his mother called Mary? And are not his brothers James and Joseph and Simon and Judas? And are not all his sisters with us? Where then did this man get all this?"*

Obviously, he must not have expressed much of that power as a young man or the hometown people wouldn't have seemed so surprised. It is likely he didn't come into his full power until the experience in the desert when he surrendered completely to the Christ level of mind.

In Matthew 28:18, he says, *"...All authority in heaven and on earth has been given to me."* Talking about crucifixion and resurrection, he says in John 10:17,18, *"I lay down my life... No one takes it from me, but I lay it down of my own accord. I have power to lay it down, and I have power to take it up again. I have received this command from my father."*

His access to this power was experienced through his indwelling Christ nature, which had come into full expression. He was spiritually awake—and of course ones does a great deal more awake than asleep!

In this spiritually awake condition, Jesus knew that his will and God's will were one and the same. He recognized the activity of God in every situation and condition of life. He would take a final step that demonstrated the eternal and indestructible nature of the Christ consciousness, and in so doing would introduce the next step of evolution to the human race. When he said, *"You will see the Son of Man seated at the right hand of the Power and coming with the clouds of heaven"* (Mark 14:62), Jesus was referring not just to himself but to the Christ potential in every person who experiences the transformation.

To initiate this next step of human evolution and to complete his mission, Jesus needed to take that step himself. And he couldn't take it unless he was actually making it possible for others to do so at the same time. In other words, to experience Christ power and glory, one must help bring it to others. And to bring it to others, one must experience Christ power and glory. Jesus' mission and gift were immutably tied together in an evolutionary dance. This is why Step Twelve requires us to "carry this message to others."

Every human being in this process has a unique and personal way to assist others and, through that, all of humankind in the journey to spiritual awakening. We will discuss that later in this chapter. Right now, it is sufficient to know that Christ power is not available to individuals unless they are willing to actively help others find it as well.

Let's consider for a moment the activity of God as expressed in Jesus' mission and within the culture and society in which he lived. He indicated that the divine presence could be found even in his "enemies." For example, he made a statement to the effect that God was involved in the seeming power that Pontius Pilate had over his life.

Pilate therefore said to him, "Do you refuse to speak to me? Do you not know that I have power to release you, and power to crucify you?" Jesus answered him, "You would have no power over me unless it had been given you from above." (John 19:10)

This passage is often used to support the idea that God required Jesus to be sacrificed for the sins of humanity. Considering that God created humanity and did so in a way He described as "very good," this idea of retribution simply doesn't make sense.

And if Jesus' death was supposed to reduce human suffering, well, it doesn't seem to have been very effective. If anything, science seems to have been much more responsible for the reduction of human suffering than the Christian church has been over the past few hundred years. (Having said that, I need to add that I truly believe the church has done the best it could, and in many cases that has been considerable.)

Another explanation is much more consistent with Jesus' life, our evolving nature, and Jesus' disclosures about the real nature of the salvation he brought. Hopefully, by now you can see that the answer lies in the understanding of his mission and the way God intended to accomplish it.

The crucifixion and resurrection were important elements of Jesus' mission. It may be that his physical death was required—but not as a sacrifice. In initiating the next step in human evolution, he needed to make a demonstration that would leave no question about God's power and the eternal nature of life and love expressed through the Christ.

That demonstration needed to be completed within the existing state of human nature. Under the most trying circumstances, Jesus maintained access to divine strength. He resisted the temptation to use Christ power against anyone, no matter how threatening the situation.

According to the scriptures, the only times Jesus ever attempted to use force was in the purification of the temple. In those cases, he attempted to use human power, not divine, and, evidently wasn't very successful.

In the temple he found people selling cattle, sheep, and doves, and the money-changers seated at their tables. Making a whip of cords, he drove all of them out of the temple, both the sheep and the cattle. He also poured out the coins of the money-changers and overturned their tables. He told those who were selling the doves, "Take these things out of here! Stop making my Father's house a marketplace!"

His disciples remembered that it was written, "Zeal for your house will consume me." The Jews then said to him, "What sign can you show us for doing this?" Jesus answered them, "Destroy this temple, and in three days I will raise it up." The Jews then said, "This temple has been under construction for forty-six years, and will you raise it up in three days?" But he was speaking of the temple of his

119

body. After he was raised from the dead, his disciples remembered that he had said this; and they believed the scripture and the word that Jesus had spoken. (John 2:13-22)

Jesus regularly pointed out how the religious power structure was misrepresenting the nature of the God/human relationship. He knew that his words and actions would be threatening to religious authorities and that they would ultimately be forced to kill him. But Jesus did not try to force change. He knew that if he stayed focused on the truth, God's presence would express itself—even through the actions of those who viewed him as an enemy.

The "villains" of this story—Judas, Herod, and Pilate—were inextricably immersed in the evolution process whether they were aware of it or not. Deep within their life energy, at the deepest unconscious level, there existed the unified forward movement of God. They all played the roles consistent with the current state of human nature. Jesus knew they would, enabling him to take the step that would eventually bring a new reality and a new world to all humanity.

Jesus took on the ultimate resistance in order to make the ultimate demonstration. He did so in order to authentically address any doubts as to whether or not worldly resistance could adversely affect spiritual evolution when an individual has the right mindset. *Let the same mind be in you that was in Christ Jesus.* (Philippians 2:5)

Thankfully, few of us will ever have to deal with the degree of resistance Jesus took on. But we all encounter some kind of resistance, either from within or without. From without, it often comes in the form of people or circumstances over which we have little control. From within, it can take the form of negative thinking, disease, habitual fear-based reactions to life, addictions, or low self-esteem.

For most people there doesn't seem to be any shortage of circumstances or conditions that can cause problems, and they all seem to keep us locked in the prison of human limitation. The key now is to adopt the perspective Jesus had—that adversity can and always will be transcended by our emerging Christ nature whenever we make that our purpose.

Dealing with the resistance that comes from within may be more difficult because it seems so much a part of us. But if internal resistance is a problem, using the earlier inventory and forgiveness steps will always work. This step addresses that by stating our need to "practice these principles in all our affairs."

Great power exists in knowing that God is active in every situation and condition in our lives and that God's activity supports our evolution at every moment. Knowing that and responding to life based on that truth quickens our spiritual growth. This is a powerful state of mind, one in which you and God become masters of your world. Christ then becomes the Lord of your being. From this perspective, power takes on a whole new meaning.

Surprisingly enough, what we call human power can actually be enhanced by certain spiritual practices. (Maybe that shouldn't be surprising, knowing that evolution is really a gradual process in which the new builds on what is already present.) Meditation and visualization have been shown to improve concentration, effectiveness, and health. Affirmations and controlled positive thinking also can bring positive results. People have used these practices to gain a degree of power over their lives, to increase their capacity to function successfully in the world, and to become much better competitors.

Competition of all kinds—whether on the playing field, in the corporate world, or in politics—is largely primate-based behavior. This is the human way and it certainly is not wrong. The important thing is not to get locked into it as the only way. There is a divine way that will eventually transcend and replace it.

The point here is to understand how ego-based human power can be temporarily increased through the application of spiritual practices. Christ power is complete. It cannot be increased. It can only be released. There is a big difference between increasing power and releasing power.

That is one of the main differentiating characteristics between the two. Human power can be increased in many ways—through such things as training, diet, conditioning, and mental/spiritual practices. That is good, but it also is very important to know that efforts to develop human power can impede the process of accessing Christ power.

Successful competition and pride are often the primate/ego-based motives for those who successfully develop human power. Watch a football tailback's reaction after sprinting into the end zone. In win/lose situations, pride in winning is a temptation that's obviously hard to resist!

Many people are at the stage of evolution where this is very appropriate and rewarding for their lives, and most people would say you shouldn't pass up this kind of satisfaction. There's nothing wrong with that, but don't confuse it with spiritual power. They are not the same.

One of Jesus' most important—and radical—talks addressed the issue of human power. It is that part of the Sermon on the Mount known as the Beatitudes. A short version of it can be found in Matthew, 5:3-12.

> *Blessed are the poor in spirit, for theirs is the kingdom of heaven.*
> *Blessed are those who mourn, for they will be comforted.*
> *Blessed are the meek, for they will inherit the earth.*
> *Blessed are those who hunger and thirst for righteousness, for they will be filled.*
> *Blessed are the merciful, for they will receive mercy.*
> *Blessed are the pure in heart, for they will see God.*
> *Blessed are the peacemakers, for they will be called children of God.*
> *Blessed are those who are persecuted for righteousness' sake, for theirs is the kingdom of heaven.*
> *Blessed are you when people revile you and persecute you and utter all kinds of evil against you falsely on my account.*
> *Rejoice and be glad, for your reward is great in heaven, for in the same way they persecuted the prophets who were before you.*

Jesus is saying here that people who are not considered very powerful in human terms will find it easier to enter into the next step of evolution. In fact, he clearly implies that efforts to develop human power will delay entry into the promised kingdom.

It is, of course, exceptionally hard to give up winning. But Jesus makes the point very clear in his teachings. In Matthew 19:30, he says: *"But many who are first will be last, and the last will be first."* Those who possess and value high status, rank, or power will have to wait until their human power is diminished.

Does this mean we must sacrifice all positions of leadership or other highly successful roles in order to experience Christ power? Absolutely not! But, it does mean we will not use human power in conflict or win/lose competition to gain those positions. Our roles will be divinely ordained to serve the movement of evolution. Position and prestige and the powers associated with it are not the issue—service is.

Though Christ power cannot be increased, that doesn't mean you and I might not be called to training or education in order to best express our unique gifts. But this will be different. To a great extent, these efforts will be free of the pressures associated with success or failure that are nearly always part of the ego's effort to develop human power.

Curiously, most people who enter religious ministry through an ordination program feel a great deal of pressure regarding success or failure. I certainly did early on. Success/failure anxiety made me question whether I was answering a true calling or simply making another attempt to gain satisfaction and recognition of my worthiness.

Looking at it with honesty, I realized the answer was "yes" to both possibilities. My calling was indeed genuine. At the same time, I was attempting to struggle my way to success, watching out for situations, conditions, or people whose self-interests might threaten my chances.

I'm sure that is how most people get into ministry. Little wonder why some get into trouble, and little wonder why there is strife in so many churches. Strife and conflict are always based on primate/human competitive or conflicting self-interest, often with the desire for success and the best interests of the church in the hearts of all involved. And usually, the minister is right in the middle of it all.

Today, I feel I have surrendered much of that fear and struggle. For the most part, I feel free. The required work I do is much easier. I am not as easily threatened. I get along with people much better, and there is certainly value in that for a person serving in a spiritual leadership role.

I know I am not completely there yet, but I am on the way and I am to the place where I truly like the trip most of the time. Life is getting easier and much more satisfying. God power is accomplishing more and more, in and through me.

As I have said, Christ power cannot be developed or acquired. It is already present, complete and perfected. It can only emerge in and through a human consciousness that has become receptive, that is free of fear enough to let the Christ power have its way. Christ power is always a gift, a condition that emerges naturally and partly due to our conscious efforts in the transformation process.

As we lose the urge to compete or participate in conflicts of self-interest and as we become aware of the fundamental truth that all life energy supports the next step in our evolution, we begin to access Christ power in our own unique and wonderful ways. Life becomes good! That's what the "good news" of the gospels is about.

Through the Twelve Steps we have a way to make that "good news" visible as the stories of our lives. Thank You, God!

Summary

CONTINUING THE JOURNEY

If you have completed these Twelve Steps, hopefully you have discovered your mission and your particular gifts and have made a commitment to them, at least to some degree. You now know that all the satisfaction that could be desired in life is available through expression of those gifts in ways that further the evolution into Christ consciousness. You have begun losing the fear of not having enough of what is needed to experience life abundantly.

If this is your experience, you have also discovered that your mission and your gifts are divinely ordained. God has chosen to bless you with these gifts and to bless the world with you. God will support you—life will support you—as your gifts are gloriously expressed through the Christ in you.

When we begin to enter into Christ consciousness, meditation and prayer bring about ideas, images, and descriptions of what life is to be. They come into expression not through struggle but through relaxed, enthusiastic activity, and watchful mindfulness. Watchful mindfulness is a state of mind that recognizes the universal power of an active God. Intuition tells you where to look in the world for opportunities. It also tells you where to turn and when to act, all in accordance with the way God works in supporting your mission in life.

It would be tempting to try to describe what it will be like for you as you experience this new state of being. But I can't, because it will be different for us all.

Each person will experience the Christ uniquely as it emerges through individual personalities, talents, abilities, and circumstances of life. The one thing I do know is that you are exactly right for the process. You do not have to acquire any more talents, abilities, or virtues in order for this transformation to happen to you. You are, like Jesus was, the right human being at the right time, in the right place, with the right people in your life.

The kind of work you will be called to do—the way your gift will serve you and the world—will be just right for you. Certainly not everyone will become professional clergy. Different people will do many wonderful and varied things that serve the human condition and its evolution. Most professions and occupations can be divinely assimilated into this evolutionary experience. You do not have to change anything unless directed to do so by the Holy Spirit.

Even so, everyone must be a minister of sorts. New spiritual communities will be made up of individuals who understand and participate in the evolutionary process. They know they cannot evolve into Christ consciousness and access divine power without authentically serving in ways that support others in the transformation experience. They know that all human life energy is one and that anyone who is evolving must help evolve all of it.

In short, unless you and I help the human race in its evolution we cannot experience our own. And unless we experience our own, we cannot provide any real help to the human race. That was the truth Jesus taught and demonstrated in his own life, in relationships with his disciples, and in his relationship with us through the Scriptures and the Holy Spirit. So if your evolution into Christ consciousness brings you into new and exciting endeavors in the business world, the professional world, or any other world, in order to continue you must be actively involved in some form of spiritual community that helps others who are ready.

This experience in the spiritual community will be one of the most rewarding ways you spend your time and energy. Your specific ministerial role will be determined by the emerging Christ in you and will fit perfectly with the roles others are playing in that community.

Through God's loving presence you will be given the perfect way to support and be supported by that ministry. Listening to the perfect council of the indwelling Christ, you will be guided to share your time, talent, and treasure in ways that demonstrate God's abundant support of your transformation and that of others.

To be sure, we are all unique individuals. But I honestly believe every one of us shares a common goal in life. That may sound presumptuous, but it really isn't. It is actually what Jesus said.

Consider the fact that every human being has the same ultimate desire, which is to be as fully human as possible. That's true enough, isn't it? I believe, as Jesus said, that all human beings—and especially those who are emerging into this new awareness—should have as their only goal the transformation into Christ consciousness. In that goal you and I will certainly walk singular paths and have singular objectives along the way. But our goal is the same: conscious union of our minds with the mind of God.

The birth of our Christ sense of self and our entrance into the Kingdom of God/Heaven must be the one and only goal. In Matthew 6:33, Jesus said: *"But strive first for the kingdom of God and his righteousness, and all these things will be given to you as well."*

Let it be so for you. Let us become conscious of our unity with God, with all life, and with each other as we join in meaningful and satisfying relationships of mutual enhancement. And let us continue the journey together.

Barry Vennard

SELECTED BIBLIOGRAPHY

For the reader's reference, here are a few of the works that were influential in the development of ideas expressed in this book.

Alcoholics Anonymous World Services Inc. *Alcoholics Anonymous.* (3rd ed., 1976)

Alcoholics Anonymous World Services Inc. *Twelve Steps and Twelve Traditions.* (1981)

Behe, M. *Darwin's Black Box. Touchstone Books (1998)*

Behe, M. & Dembski, W. *Intelligent Design.* Intervarsity Press (1999)

Brinkley, D. & Perry, P. *Saved by the Light: The True Story of a Man Who Died Twice and the Profound Revelations He Received.* Harper Mass Market Paperbacks (1995)

Darwin, C. *The Origin of Species.* Grammercy (1998)

Dawkins, R. *The Selfish Gene.* Oxford Press (1990)

De Waal, F. *Good Natured: The Origins of Right and Wrong in Humans and Other Animals.* Harvard Press (1997)

De Waal, F. *Chimpanzee Politics.* John Hopkins University Press (2000)

De Waal, F. *Tree of Origins, What Primate Behavior Can Tell Us about Human Social Evolution.* Harvard Press (2001)

Dennet, D. *Darwin's Dangerous Ideas.* Touchstone Books (1996)

Diamond, J. *Guns, Germs, and Steel.* W.W. Norton & Co. (1997)

Diamond, J. *The Third Chimpanzee.* HarperTrade (1992)

129

Fillmore, C. *The Twelve Powers of Man.* Unity Village: Unity School of Christianity (1985)

Fillmore, C. *Metaphysical Bible Dictionary.* Unity Village: Unity School of Christianity (1994)

Fox, M. *Original Blessing.* Bear & Co. (1983)

Markova, D. *No Enemies Within.* Conari Press (1994)

Spong, J. *Why Christianity Must Change or Die.* Harper (1998)

Spong, J. *Rescuing the Bible from Fundamentalism.* Harper (1991)

Wilson, E.O. *The Diversity of Life.* W.W. Norton & Co. (1999)

Wright, R. Non-Zero, The Logic of Human Destiny. *Vintage Books (2001)*

ABOUT THE UNITY MOVEMENT

Unity is a Christ-based spiritual and educational movement that teaches the practical application of the spiritual principles taught and demonstrated by Jesus. It was founded on the idea that following Jesus doesn't mean worshipping him; it means coming into the same relationship he had with God. The movement, founded in the 1890s, is growing throughout the United States and the world.

Unity's founders were Charles and Myrtle Fillmore. Myrtle was a teacher, wife, and mother who found herself in the late stages of an extremely serious illness. Overwhelming feelings of powerlessness led her to attend a New Thought lecture, and what she heard there triggered the Christ potential within her. She left that lecture with a new sense of who she was.

As this potential began to emerge, it transformed her conscious mind; she knew herself as a child of God and her life changed dramatically. Under the influence of the emerging Christ, she began to focus her energy and attention on the divine presence within her rather than on the problems in her physical life.

Myrtle Fillmore experienced a complete healing, and through this new divine power she was able to initiate the healing process in many others. At the age of 86, after many years as co-leader of the Unity movement, she is said to have realized that her life activity was about to expand. That expansion would be through the process we call physical death, a process she did not resist since she had long before entered into the consciousness of eternal life.

Charles Fillmore was an entrepreneur who alternated between success and failure in business. During the time of Myrtle's experience, he was struggling in a real estate venture. As he observed his wife's transformation, he began to divert his energies away from business into an exploration of spirituality and meditation.

Charles's objective wasn't necessarily to become a better businessman, but to explore the possibilities of a conscious relationship with God. Actually, his business and the family's finances suffered as he lost interest in his previous focus. He began an intense and prolonged practice of meditation that slowly transformed his mind and his life.

The couple's combined emerging Christ natures eventually resulted in the Unity movement, which touches millions of lives today. It resulted in them living extraordinarily satisfying and meaningful lives.

ABOUT THE AUTHOR

Barry Vennard has served as the Senior Minister of the Unity Church of the Triangle in Raleigh, North Carolina and the Spiritual Leader of the Unity Church of Ames in Ames, Iowa. He has served as a minister/spiritual leader in the Unity movement for a little over eight years.

This work is inspired by the author's deep and profound spiritual experience, by twenty-five years of practicing the twelve steps, and by his search to integrate his spiritual awakening with the teachings of Jesus and scientific discovery about human origins through evolution. Some of this experience is described in the book's preface. For the last five years he has successfully taught and supported others who have found transformation of their lives through the application of these principles as presented in this book. This twelve-step program along with the inspired way the author associates the teachings of Jesus with human origins through evolution makes this book a powerful and compelling tool for personal transformation.

Printed in the United States
116016LV00002B/238-327/A

9 780759 697577